Smoothies for Beg

The Ultimate Guide to Effortless, Healthy and Tasty 4-Season Smoothies - Made Simple for Weight Loss, Energy Boost, Immune Support, Nutrient Absorption, and Body Cleansing

by
Martha Fleming

© Copyright 2024 by Martha Fleming - All rights reserved.

The following Book is reproduced below with the goal of providing information that is as accurate and reliable as possible. Regardless, purchasing this Book can be seen as consent to the fact that both the publisher and the author of this book are in no way experts on the topics discussed within and that any recommendations or suggestions that are made herein are for entertainment purposes only. Professionals should be consulted as needed prior to undertaking any of the action endorsed herein.

This declaration is deemed fair and valid by both the American Bar Association and the Committee of Publishers Association and is legally binding throughout the United States.

Furthermore, the transmission, duplication, or reproduction of any of the following work including specific information will be considered an illegal act irrespective of if it is done electronically or in print. This extends to creating a secondary or tertiary copy of the work or a recorded copy and is only allowed with the express written consent from the Publisher. All additional right reserved.

The information in the following pages is broadly considered a truthful and accurate account of facts and as such, any inattention, use, or misuse of the information in question by the reader will render any resulting actions solely under their purview. There are no scenarios in which the publisher or the original author of this work can be in any fashion deemed liable for any hardship or damages that may befall them after undertaking information described herein.

Additionally, the information in the following pages is intended only for informational purposes and should thus be thought of as universal. As befitting its nature, it is presented without assurance regarding its prolonged validity or interim quality. Trademarks that are mentioned are done without written consent and can in no way be considered an endorsement from the trademark holder.

Table Of contents

Table Of contents 5
Introduction 14
    The Art and Essence of Smoothies 14
    The Smoothie Spectrum: Varieties and Types 15
    How to Make a Perfect Smoothie 16
    Health Benefits of Smoothies 17
    Preparing Smoothies: Tools and Ingredients 18
    Smoothies for All Seasons: An Overview 20
    Consumption of Smoothies: Advice, Precautions, and General Recommendations 21
CHAPTER 1: BREAKFAST SMOOTHIE RECIPES 24
    Spring Awakening: 24
        Recipe 1: Blooming Berry Bliss 24
        Recipe 2: Green Morning Revival 24
        Recipe 3: Citrus Sunrise 24
        Recipe 4: Spring Melon Medley 24
        Recipe 5: Protein Petal Punch 25
        Recipe 6: Lavender Love Smoothie 25
        Recipe 7: Minty Pineapple Paradise 25
        Recipe 8: Choco-Banana Blossom 25
        Recipe 9: Floral Apricot Fusion 25
        Recipe 10: Omega-Raspberry Elixir 26
    Summer Mornings: 26
        Recipe 1: Tropical Sunshine Burst 26
        Recipe 2: Peachy Keen Sunrise 26
        Recipe 3: Zesty Lemon Quencher 26
        Recipe 4: Kiwi Kale Kickstart 27
        Recipe 5: Cherry Almond Bliss 27
        Recipe 6: Blueberry Basil Boost 27
        Recipe 7: Pomegranate Passion with seeds 27
        Recipe 8: Refreshing Watermelon Wave 28
        Recipe 9: Spicy Mango Tango 28

- Recipe 10: Creamy Cacao Cool-off 28

Cozy Autumn **28**

- Recipe 1: Spiced Pumpkin Pleasure 28
- Recipe 2: Apple Pie Embrace 28
- Recipe 3: Warm Ginger Zing 29
- Recipe 4: Nutty Maple Hug 29
- Recipe 5: Pear and Pecan Perfection 29
- Recipe 6: Cranberry Crimson Crush 29
- Recipe 7: Sweet Potato Sunrise 30
- Recipe 8: Fig and Honey Harmony 30
- Recipe 9: Chai Chilled Charm 30
- Recipe 10: Caramel Apple Crave 30

Winter Energy **31**

- Recipe 1: Winterberry Warmth 31
- Recipe 2: Mocha Motivator 31
- Recipe 3: Peppermint Pep 31
- Recipe 4: Spicy Ginger Glow 31
- Recipe 5: Power Matcha Mix 32
- Recipe 6: Cocoa Comfort 32
- Recipe 7: Energizing Beet Boost 32
- Recipe 8: Nutmeg Nectar 32
- Recipe 9: Guarana Gusto 33
- Recipe 10: Raspberry Revival 33

CHAPTER 2: Lunchtime Smoothie Recipes 35

Spring Greens **35**

- Recipe 1: Verdant Zest 35
- Recipe 2: Herbal Harmony 35
- Recipe 3: Green Zen 35
- Recipe 4: Spring Sprout 35
- Recipe 5: Asparagus Ascend 36
- Recipe 6: Celery Citrus Sip 36
- Recipe 7: Pea & Mint Magic 36
- Recipe 8: Watercress Wonder 36
- Recipe 9: Spring Basil Bliss 37

Summertime Joy **37**

- Recipe 1: Berry Bliss Burst 37

- Recipe 2: Mango Melody 37
- Recipe 3: Sunlit Citrus Splash 37
- Recipe 4: Kiwi & Kale Dance 38
- Recipe 5: Minty Watermelon Wave 38
- Recipe 6: Passionfruit Paradise 38
- Recipe 7: Cool Cucumber Melange 38
- Recipe 8: Papaya Peach Fusion 39
- Recipe 9: Zesty Cherry Chill 39

Autumn Harvest **39**
- Recipe 1: Autumn Maple Melody 39
- Recipe 2: Apple Orchard Delight 40
- Recipe 3: Cranberry Crush 40
- Recipe 4: Fig & Date Symphony 40
- Recipe 5: Nutty Butternut Bliss 40
- Recipe 6: Pecan Pie Smoothie 41
- Recipe 7: Golden Persimmon Potion 41
- Recipe 8: Sweet Potato Euphoria 41
- Recipe 9: Chai-infused Pear Perfection 41

Winter Wellness **42**
- Recipe 1: Immunity Boosting Blend 42
- Recipe 2: Creamy Cacao Comfort 42
- Recipe 3: Spicy Turmeric Tango 42
- Recipe 4: Gingered Pear Perfection 43
- Recipe 5: Energizing Espresso Elixir 43
- Recipe 6: Walnut Wonder with kefir 43
- Recipe 7: Berry Citrus Symphony 43
- Recipe 8: Chilly Chaga Charm 44
- Recipe 9: Avocado Almond Ambrosia 44

CHAPTER 3: Dinner Smoothie Recipes **46**

Spring Detox **46**
- Recipe 1: Green Machine Medley 46
- Recipe 2: Fresh Mint Mirage 46
- Recipe 3: Celery Serenity 46
- Recipe 4: Dandelion Delight 46
- Recipe 5: Pineapple Paradise 47
- Recipe 6: Fennel Fusion 47

Recipe 7: Beetroot Bliss 47
Recipe 8: Radiant Raspberry 47
Recipe 9: Lemon Lush 48
Recipe 10: Turmeric Twist 48

Summer Sunset **48**
Recipe 1: Tropical Harmony 48
Recipe 2: Berry Bliss with Acai 49
Recipe 3: Peachy Serenity 49
Recipe 4: Citrus Glow 49
Recipe 5: Cherry Charm with Goji 49
Recipe 6: Watermelon Whisper 50
Recipe 7: Sunset Serenade 50
Recipe 8: Apricot Euphoria 50
Recipe 9: Plum Passion 50
Recipe 10: Guava Grace 51

Fall Comfort **51**
Recipe 1: Cinnamon Apple Crisp 51
Recipe 2: Cozy Pumpkin Patch 51
Recipe 3: Pecan Pie Dream 51
Recipe 4: Sweet Potato Comfort 52
Recipe 5: Cranberry Cheer 52
Recipe 6: Toasty Hazelnut Heaven 52
Recipe 7: Fig & Date Delight 52
Recipe 8: Maple Walnut Warmth 53
Recipe 9: Pear & Ginger Soothe 53
Recipe 10: Spiced Carrot Cake 53

Winter Soothe **53**
Recipe 1: Vanilla Snowflake 53
Recipe 2: Minty Cocoa Comfort 53
Recipe 3: Citrus Winter Bliss 54
Recipe 4: Spiced Almond Joy 54
Recipe 5: Berry Winter Warmer 54
Recipe 6: Cozy Chocolate Cherry 54
Recipe 7: Nutty Caramel Hug 55
Recipe 8: Gingerbread Embrace 55
Recipe 9: Pomegranate Peace 55

Recipe 10: Caramelized Pear Whisper 55

CHAPTER 4: Weight Loss Smoothie Recipes 57

Recipe 1: Green Apple Metabolism Booster 57

Recipe 2: Berry Protein Fusion 57

Recipe 3: Citrus Fat Burner 57

Recipe 4: Spicy Avocado Slimmer 57

Recipe 5: Green Tea Metabolism Mixer 58

Recipe 6: Carrot Ginger Glow 58

Recipe 7: Tropical Turmeric Tonic 58

Recipe 8: Kale and Kiwi Kickstart 58

Recipe 9: Blueberry Blast 59

Recipe 10: Sweet Spinach Slimmer 59

Recipe 11: Minty Melon Refresh 59

Recipe 12: Protein Pumpkin Patch 60

Recipe 13: Zesty Lemon Cleanse 60

Recipe 14: Choco Almond Dream 60

Recipe 15: Beetroot Bliss 60

Recipe 16: Strawberry Basil Booster 61

Recipe 17: Apple Cinnamon Delight 61

Recipe 18: Pineapple Paradise 61

Recipe 19: Raspberry Refresher 61

Recipe 20: Savory Spinach and Avocado 62

CHAPTER 5: Energy-Boosting Smoothie Recipes 64

Recipe 1: Protein Powerhouse 64

Recipe 2: Greek Yogurt Citrus Zing 64

Recipe 3: Berry Quinoa Boost 64

Recipe 4: Spinach Tofu Energizer 64

Recipe 5: Tropical Lentil Bliss 65

Recipe 6: Almond Chickpea Fusion 65

Recipe 7: Spicy Ginger Protein Kick 65

Recipe 8: Peanut Butter Banana Delight 65

Recipe 9: Oatmeal Cinnamon Protein Rush 66

Recipe 10: Peachy Protein Power 66

Recipe 11: Kiwi Kale Edamame Charge 66

Recipe 12: Cocoa Almond Lift 66

Recipe 13: Pomegranate Pumpkin Seed Punch 67
Recipe 14: Pineapple Spirulina Surge 67
Recipe 15: Chia Cherry Charge 67
Recipe 16: Mocha Hemp Elevation 67
Recipe 17: Pineapple Tempeh Triumph 68

CHAPTER 6: Vegetarian and Vegan Smoothie Recipes 70

Recipe 1: Green Machine 70
Recipe 2: Soy Berry Bliss 70
Recipe 3: Mango Tango 70
Recipe 4: Spicy Carrot Cooler 70
Recipe 5: Walnut Wonder with banana 71
Recipe 6: Pumpkin Pleasure 71
Recipe 7: Sweet Beet Retreat 71
Recipe 8: Cacao Cashew Bliss 71
Recipe 9: Raspberry Chia Harmony 71
Recipe 10: Zesty Lime Lullaby 72
Recipe 11: Turmeric Ginger Soothe 72
Recipe 12: Avocado Aloe Elixir 72
Recipe 13: Papaya Passion 72
Recipe 14: Matcha Mint Marvel 73
Recipe 15: Blueberry Basil Burst 73
Recipe 16: Pineapple Coconut Oasis 73
Recipe 17: Golden Grapefruit Glow 73

CHAPTER 7: Cleansing Smoothie Recipes 76

Recipe 1: Citrus Cleanse 76
Recipe 2: Celery Symphony 76
Recipe 3: Ginger Glow 76
Recipe 4: Cucumber Calm 76
Recipe 5: Dandelion Detox 76
Recipe 6: Coconut Watermelon Wave 77
Recipe 7: Kale Kickstart 77
Recipe 8: Charcoal Clarity 77
Recipe 9: Pineapple Purity 77
Recipe 10: Fennel Freshness 78
Recipe 11: Spirulina Surge 78

Recipe 12: Acai Awakening 78

Recipe 13: Turmeric Tonic 78

Recipe 14: Beetroot Bliss 79

Recipe 15: Parsley Purity 79

Recipe 16: Goji Grapefruit Goodness 79

Recipe 17: Matcha Magic 79

CHAPTER 8: Gluten-Free Smoothie Recipes 81

Recipe 1: Simple Berry Bliss 81

Recipe 2: Choco-Almond Delight 81

Recipe 3: Citrus Symphony 81

Recipe 4: Avocado Serenity 81

Recipe 5: Pistachio Pleasure 81

Recipe 6: Strawberry Sunrise 82

Recipe 7: Hazelnut Harmony 82

Recipe 8: Kiwi Kiss 82

Recipe 9: Peach Perfection 82

Recipe 10: Tropical Triumph 83

Recipe 11: Vanilla Velvet 83

Recipe 12: Raspberry Rapture 83

Recipe 13: Lychee Luxury 83

Recipe 14: Cashew Charm 83

Recipe 15: Blueberry Burst 84

Recipe 16: Pomegranate Purity 84

Recipe 17: Cinnamon Cradle 84

CHAPTER 9: Lactose-Free Smoothie Recipes 86

Recipe 1: Honey Berry Bliss 86

Recipe 2: Tropical Zest 86

Recipe 3: Minty Cucumber Refresher 86

Recipe 4: Spicy Ginger Pineapple 86

Recipe 5: Pomegranate Passion with juice 87

Recipe 6: Kiwi Quencher 87

Recipe 7: Peachy Keen 87

Recipe 8: Watermelon Wonder 87

Recipe 9: Apricot Almond Elixir 87

Recipe 10: Choco-Hazelnut Delight 88

Recipe 11: Pear-Fection 88

Recipe 12: Lemon-Lime Lift 88

Recipe 13: Raspberry Rhapsody 88

Recipe 14: Avocado Allure 89

Recipe 15: Vanilla Cherry Charm 89

Recipe 16: Fig Fantasy 89

Recipe 17: Plum Perfection 89

CHAPTER 10. 15 Detoxifying Daily Exercises 92

Daily exercises to enhance the detox effects of smoothies 92

1. Gentle Morning Yoga Stretch 92

2. Midday Breathing Meditation 93

3. Evening Walk and Twist 93

4. Dynamic Lunges 94

5. Nightly Gratitude Journaling and Stretching 94

6. Morning Sun Salutations 95

7. Hydrating Aqua Aerobics 95

8. Deep Stretching and Foam Rolling 95

9. Energizing Dance Cardio 96

10. Tranquil Evening Tai Chi 96

11. Dynamic High-Intensity Interval Training (HIIT) 97

12. Gentle Pilates Core Workout 98

13. Restorative Evening Walk 98

14. Meditative Breathing Exercises 99

15. Strength-Building Bodyweight Exercises 100

CHAPTER 11 - 4-Week Detoxifying Meal Plan and Preparation 102

Conversion table 109

INDEX (Alphabetical Order) 111

Before you start reading, Scan this QR Code to get your Bonus content!

Introduction

The Art and Essence of Smoothies

The mere mention of the word "smoothie" brings to mind a refreshing, flavorful concoction, artfully blending taste and nutrition in a single glass. Much like a symphony, every smoothie is an orchestration of ingredients that speaks directly to our senses. Let's dive into the vibrant world of smoothies, where every sip explores flavor, tradition, and well-being.

The journey of smoothies is as fascinating as the flavors they encompass. The concept of blending fruits and other nutritious elements is not new and can be traced back centuries. Indigenous cultures, long before modern blenders, muddled fruits and nuts together to create nourishing, energy-boosting concoctions. However, the smoothies as we know them today have their roots in the 20th-century United States. The invention of electric blenders laid the foundation for this beloved drink, allowing creativity to thrive in a cup.

As time progressed, smoothies evolved from a simple blend of fruits and milk to an eclectic mix that could cater to various palates and health needs. From the West Coast's health-conscious communities to the bustling streets of New York, the love for smoothies surged and so did their varieties. They became not just a nutritious beverage but a canvas for innovation, allowing individuals to infuse their personality and health goals into each creation.

Smoothies, in their vibrant hues and myriad flavors, have struck a chord with a diverse and dynamic audience. For the urban professional, rushing from one meeting to another, a smoothie is a quick fix – an elixir of energy that fits perfectly into their fast-paced life. On the other hand, the health-conscious parent finds in smoothies a secret weapon to ensure her children are getting the nutrition they need, disguised in delightful flavors.

In every sip, there's an inherent promise of a healthier, more balanced lifestyle. A fitness enthusiast might share a picture of their protein-packed smoothie on Instagram, subtly influencing their network towards healthier choices. The versatility of smoothies has allowed them to seamlessly blend into diverse lifestyles, serving as a testament to their cultural significance.

Smoothies represent a perfect amalgamation of taste and health, an art form that speaks the universal language of wellness. They offer a bridge to better health without compromising on taste, appealing to the intrinsic human desire for flavors that are both delightful and nourishing. They've become a cultural icon, embodying the modern quest for a fulfilling and healthy life.

In essence, smoothies are not just a beverage; they are a phenomenon, an experience, and a representation of contemporary health culture. Their journey from the rudimentary blends of ancient times to the sophisticated concoctions of today mirrors our own evolution towards seeking wellness without forsaking pleasure.

In the following chapters, we will delve deeper into the spectrum of smoothies, unraveling their types, the secrets to crafting the perfect blend, and the health benefits they promise. But at the heart of it all, smoothies, in their simplicity and complexity, remain a testament to the fact that the quest for health and taste can coexist harmoniously in a single glass.

The Smoothie Spectrum: Varieties and Types

Navigating the landscape of smoothies reveals a delightful range tailored to various health goals and taste preferences.

Fruit Smoothies:

Fruit smoothies are a delightful mix of flavors and energy. Incorporating fruits such as mangoes, strawberries, and apples, these beverages serve as an energy boost that's both refreshing and palatable. For an urban professional rushing to meet her daily targets or a parent ensuring that the children consume their daily fruit intake, fruit smoothies are convenient and flavorful.

Vegetable Smoothies:

Vegetable smoothies serve as a convenient means of incorporating greens into a diet. Often blended with fruits to enhance the flavor, ingredients like spinach, kale, and celery can aid those focused on detoxification and weight loss.

Protein Smoothies:

For those on a quest to build muscle, protein smoothies are an essential ally. Incorporating protein powders, Greek yogurt, or nut butter, these smoothies help in muscle recovery and satiety, making them a staple for fitness enthusiasts.

The art of making a smoothie also involves fine-tuning its texture and flavor to cater to diverse palates.

Achieving Creaminess:

The texture of a smoothie can make or break the experience. The creaminess achieved by adding a banana, avocado, or yogurt can transform a quick meal into a satisfying feast. It's a clever way for parents to ensure the health-packed glass is met with eager hands.

A Burst of Freshness:

The freshness of citrus fruits can uplift a smoothie's profile, giving it a refreshing quality. Adding orange or a dash of lemon juice provides a burst of freshness that can be invigorating.

Balancing Flavors:

Flavor balancing is key. The sweetness of a ripe mango can cut through the grassy taste of spinach, creating a blend that's both tasty and nutritious. Such combinations are perfect for those introducing healthier food options to their family or seeking to enjoy their nutritional journey.

Understanding the varieties and types of smoothies is crucial for tailoring them to specific needs and goals. Whether the aim is to lose weight, gain health, or simply find quick and tasty recipes, the diverse spectrum of smoothies offers options for everyone. By considering the classification and the balance of textures and flavors, one can craft smoothies that are not just beverages but experiences tailored to health goals and taste preferences.

How to Make a Perfect Smoothie

Creating the perfect smoothie is akin to crafting a personalized wellness potion. The seamless blend of ingredients, each thoughtfully chosen, not only satisfies the taste buds but also serves as a nutrient-packed meal in a glass. Achieving that perfection, however, requires an understanding of basic proportions and techniques, along with some handy tips to fine-tune the consistency.

Embarking on the journey to create a perfect smoothie begins with mastering the basic proportions. Imagine a busy urban professional, stealing a few minutes from her hectic schedule, who seeks to whip up a quick yet nourishing smoothie. She needs to know just how much of each ingredient will create that tantalizing blend.

A classic rule of thumb is to maintain a ratio of 1:1 between the base liquid and the solid ingredients. About a cup of liquid — be it almond milk for the lactose-intolerant or refreshing coconut water for that tropical zing — forms the foundation. Adding an equal portion of solid ingredients like fruits, vegetables, or protein powders ensures a balanced taste and texture.

The layering of flavors is an art. Begin with mild flavors and gradually introduce the robust ones. A base of mild spinach can be enhanced with the sweetness of a banana, while a scoop of protein powder ensures that the smoothie packs a punch in terms of nutrition.

Crafting Perfection: Tips for Achieving the Perfect Consistency

Consistency is the secret ingredient that transforms a good smoothie into a perfect one. A mother, trying to introduce her kids to healthier eating habits, knows that the drink needs to be just the right texture to appeal to young palates.

Adjusting Thickness:

The thickness of a smoothie can be adjusted to personal preference. Adding more liquid can thin out a too-thick blend, while ingredients like chia seeds or oats can be introduced to thicken a runny mix.

Temperature and Flavor:

The temperature of your ingredients matters. Using frozen fruits or a handful of ice can result in a cool, refreshing smoothie, ideal for an instant energy lift.

The Art of Blending:

The blending technique also influences the final product. Start slowly to break down the ingredients and gradually increase the speed to avoid air bubbles, ensuring a silky-smooth texture.

Quality over Quantity:

Lastly, remember that quality trumps quantity. Using fresh, high-quality ingredients can make a difference in taste and nutritional value.

In essence, crafting the perfect smoothie is a harmonious blend of science and art. By understanding the basic proportions, experimenting with flavors, and fine-tuning the consistency, one can create a range of smoothies tailored to various needs. Whether it's for a busy professional seeking a quick nutritious fix, a fitness enthusiast aiming for muscle gain or a parent ensuring a balanced diet for their children, mastering the art of the perfect smoothie can be an empowering and delicious journey.

Health Benefits of Smoothies

Smoothies have become the go-to solution for individuals looking for a quick, nutritious, and tasty meal option. By blending various ingredients, they provide a concentrated dose of essential nutrients. Fruits and vegetables, often the base of smoothies, are rich in vitamins, minerals, and fiber. For instance, a smoothie with spinach offers a healthy dose of iron and Vitamin A, while a splash of citrus provides a surge of Vitamin C.

The tech-savvy professional, on a quest to find healthier eating habits, might opt for a smoothie enriched with protein through Greek yogurt or protein powder. It's not just about building muscles; protein is crucial for cellular repair and boosting immunity.

Healthy fats from avocados, chia seeds, or nuts can also be incorporated. These are not only satiating but also essential for brain health. Additionally, by opting for low-fat or plant-based milk, you can tailor the smoothie to meet your dietary needs.

In pursuing health, smoothies can play a significant role in addressing various wellness goals. They're customizable, allowing you to add ingredients that support your specific objectives.

For those looking to lose weight, smoothies provide a convenient method of portion control. A well-constructed smoothie offers a fulfilling meal without unnecessary calories. By carefully selecting ingredients like berries, leafy greens, and a lean protein source, one can craft a drink that aligns perfectly with weight loss goals.

Conversely, for individuals looking to build muscle, smoothies can be a source of energy and protein. Incorporating ingredients known for their protein content, like protein powder, Greek yogurt, or even a scoop of peanut butter, can turn a simple smoothie into a muscle-building aid.

Detoxification is another aspect where smoothies shine. By including natural detoxifying ingredients like ginger, lemon, or beetroot, a smoothie can support the body's natural cleansing processes.

For parents aiming to introduce healthier food options to their families, smoothies offer a way to sneak in a variety of nutrients in a tasty package. Kids might be hesitant to try kale or spinach on a plate, but blend it with some flavorful fruits, and it becomes a treat.

Moreover, smoothies can be a quick and easy recipe for those with time constraints. With just a few ingredients and a good blender, a nutrient-packed meal can be prepared in minutes.

The affordability and availability of smoothie ingredients make them accessible to a broad audience. From fresh fruits to frozen options, or even powdered supplements, one can always find something that fits the budget and nutritional needs.

In conclusion, the health benefits of smoothies are vast and versatile. They are a convenient, customizable, and nutritious option that can cater to a wide array of health and dietary needs. From losing weight and building muscle to detoxifying the body and ensuring a tasty, nutritious meal, smoothies can do it all in a delicious, easy-to-prepare manner.

Preparing Smoothies: Tools and Ingredients

When it comes to crafting a perfect smoothie, the first step is ensuring you have the right tools on hand. Whether you're an urban professional in need of a quick nutrient boost or a parent keen on sneaking veggies into your kid's diet, the right equipment is key.

Blenders: Your most trusted companion in this journey is a good blender. Powerful blenders can pulverize fruits, vegetables, ice, and nuts into a creamy, smooth concoction. Options range from high-end blenders, which offer various features and speed settings, to personal-sized blenders, which are compact and convenient for on-the-go lifestyles.

Cups and Containers: The choice of cups and containers is essential, especially for those who are always on the move. Selecting a durable and portable cup that can withstand the rigors of daily life while keeping your smoothie fresh is crucial.

Straws and Utensils: Reusable straws and long spoons can come in handy. A wide straw is perfect for thicker smoothies, ensuring you can enjoy every bit without any hassle.

Measuring Tools: Though smoothie-making isn't an exact science, having measuring cups and spoons can be helpful to ensure consistency, especially when you're trying to monitor calorie intake or adhere to a specific diet plan.

Picking fresh, high-quality ingredients is as pivotal as having the right tools. The ingredients you choose should align with your goals, whether it's weight loss, muscle gain, detox, or simply introducing a burst of energy into your day.

Fruits and Vegetables: Fresh produce is the backbone of any smoothie. Opt for seasonal fruits and veggies to ensure freshness and cost-effectiveness. The urban professional might prefer to have a mix of frozen fruits on hand for convenience.

Proteins: Protein powders, Greek yogurt, or nut butter are great add-ins. The choice depends on your dietary preferences and health goals. For instance, a gym enthusiast might lean towards a protein-packed smoothie post-workout.

Liquids: The choice of liquid base - be it water, dairy milk, or a plant-based alternative like almond milk - can alter the taste and nutritional content of your smoothie. Plant-based milks are often favored for being lower in calories and accommodating dietary restrictions.

Sweeteners and Flavors: While fruits often provide enough sweetness, some might prefer an extra dash of honey, agave, or a sprinkle of cinnamon. These not only enhance the flavor but can also offer additional health benefits.

Superfoods and Supplements: For those looking to amp up the nutritional content, ingredients like chia seeds, flaxseeds, or spirulina can be subtle additions.

Texture Enhancers: Ingredients like oats, avocado, or even silken tofu can elevate the creaminess of your smoothie, making it more satisfying.

In conclusion, crafting the perfect smoothie is a blend of choosing the right tools and selecting fresh, quality ingredients that align with your health goals. From the busy professional to the health-conscious parent to a fitness enthusiast, smoothies can be personalized as unique and versatile as the individuals crafting them. By prioritizing quality and freshness in ingredients and ensuring you're equipped with the necessary tools, you're well on your way to enjoying the perfect smoothie tailored just for you.

Smoothies for All Seasons: An Overview

A smoothie can be as refreshing as a spring breeze or as cozy as a warm winter blanket, capturing the essence of the seasons in a glass. To align your health journey with the rhythm of nature, it's essential to adapt your smoothie recipes to the bounty each season provides.

As the seasons change, so do our body's nutritional needs, cravings, and moods. Adapting your smoothie recipes to these changes isn't just about availability; it's about harnessing the nutritional peak of ingredients and tuning into a natural harmony with your surroundings.

Spring brings a renewal of energy. Imagine a smoothie capturing this essence with a blend of fresh greens such as spinach and kale, coupled with the vibrant sweetness of strawberries or mangoes.

Summer demands refreshment and hydration. Picture a smoothie that cools you down, combining the hydrating powers of watermelon and cucumber with a hint of mint.

Fall is a season of warmth and comfort. A smoothie crafted with spiced pumpkin or creamy sweet potato can be the perfect companion as the leaves change color.

Winter, often harsh and cold, calls for immune-boosting ingredients. Citrus fruits, rich in vitamin C, combined with ginger and a touch of honey, create a smoothie that's both comforting and protective.

Utilizing seasonal ingredients is a savvy and sustainable approach. For the urban professional seeking health through tasty and easy-to-prepare smoothies, or a parent ensuring a balanced diet for their kids, embracing the seasonality of produce provides peak flavor and nutritional value.

Seasonal produce is often more affordable and accessible, meeting the needs of those seeking cost-effective options. It also supports local farming communities, aligning with the values of conscious consumers.

Adapting to seasons doesn't mean limiting your creativity. Spring invites you to experiment with fresh berries and tender greens. Summer offers a palette of hydrating fruits and refreshing herbs. Fall brings root vegetables and warming spices to the forefront, while winter provides an array of citrus fruits.

In each season, incorporating appropriate superfoods or supplements can elevate the health benefits of your smoothie. Spirulina might add a burst of energy to a spring green smoothie, while a spoonful of chia seeds in a fall pumpkin smoothie could provide the comforting fullness we often crave.

In essence, crafting a seasonal smoothie is akin to composing a symphony, where each ingredient plays a note in harmony with your health goals. Whether you seek detoxification, energy, or a simple, tasty delight, a smoothie attuned to the season can be your daily ally. So, as you blend your way through the year, let the seasons guide your choices, ensuring each sip is a celebration of the moment.

Consumption of Smoothies: Advice, Precautions, and General Recommendations

Smoothies are more than just a convenient meal or a refreshing drink; they are a versatile canvas for health and well-being. Knowing when and how to consume them, along with certain precautions, can optimize the benefits they offer.

The timing and manner of consuming smoothies can be tailored to your individual goals and daily routines.

Morning Boost: Starting your day with a nutrient-dense smoothie can provide a sustained energy release. For those aiming to build muscle, incorporating protein sources such as Greek yogurt or protein powder can kickstart your metabolism.

Pre-Workout Fuel: Consuming a smoothie about 30 minutes before exercising can be beneficial. Ingredients like bananas can provide a quick energy boost without weighing you down.

Post-Workout Recovery: A smoothie rich in proteins and antioxidants can help muscle recovery. Berries and a scoop of protein powder can be ideal in this scenario.

Snack Substitute: For those looking to lose weight or maintain a healthy diet, substituting unhealthy snacks with a fiber-rich smoothie can be both satisfying and nutritious.

Family Meals: Smoothies can also be integrated into family meals as a healthy option, ensuring kids receive their daily dose of fruits and vegetables in a tasty manner.

Precautions and Advice

While smoothies can be a treasure trove of nutrition, it's important to consume them mindfully.

Balanced Ingredients: It's easy to turn a smoothie into a calorie bomb by adding too many high-sugar ingredients. Striking a balance between fruits, vegetables, proteins, and fats ensures you gain health without unwanted weight.

Watch the Sugar: Even natural sugars from fruits can add up quickly. To avoid overconsumption, consider mixing fruits with low-sugar vegetables like spinach or kale.

Portion Control: The convenience of smoothies can sometimes lead to overindulgence. Being mindful of portion sizes is crucial, especially for those focused on weight management.

Allergies and Interactions: Individuals with food allergies or those on specific medications should be cautious about the ingredients they use. For example, someone on blood thinners should consult a healthcare professional before adding greens like kale, which can interact with the medication.

Variety is Key: Rotating ingredients ensures you don't miss out on different nutrients and keeps your taste buds excited. The urban professional seeking fast and easy recipes will find that experimenting with different flavors can be both fun and rewarding.

Quality of Ingredients: Lastly, using fresh, quality ingredients is vital. Choosing seasonal and locally-sourced produce not only supports community farmers but also ensures that your smoothie is packed with flavor and nutrients.

In conclusion, when incorporated thoughtfully into one's diet, smoothies can be a powerful tool to meet a variety of health and lifestyle goals. By paying attention to timing, ingredient selection, and portion sizes, you can ensure that your smoothie habit is aligned with your aspirations, whether building a muscular physique, introducing healthier options to your family, or simply improving your overall health.

As the journey through this book begins, it's a collective venture where each reader's exploration adds a unique touch to the world of smoothies.

CHAPTER 1: BREAKFAST SMOOTHIE RECIPES

Spring Awakening:

Recipe 1: Blooming Berry Bliss

Prep time: 5 min
Components: 1 cup mixed berries, 1 tbsp chia seeds, 1 cup almond milk, 1 tsp agave syrup
Serves: 1
Cooking technique: Blending
Steps: Combine mixed berries, chia seeds, almond milk, and agave syrup in a blender. Process until the mixture is smooth.
Nutritional composition: Fat: 4g, Protein: 3g, Carbs: 31g, Fiber: 7g, Vitamin C, Omega-3s, Antioxidants
Calories: 180

Recipe 2: Green Morning Revival

Prep time: 5 min
Components: 1 cup spinach, ½ banana, 1 tbsp flaxseeds, 1 cup coconut water
Serves: 1
Cooking technique: Blending
Steps: Place spinach, banana, flaxseeds, and coconut water into the blender. Blend until a homogenous and smooth mixture is achieved.
Nutritional composition: Fat: 2g, **Protein:** 3g, Carbs: 25g, Fiber: 5g, Electrolytes, Vitamin A, Vitamin C
Calories: 150

Recipe 3: Citrus Sunrise

Prep time: 6 min
Components: 1 orange (peeled), ½ grapefruit (peeled), 1 tsp honey, 1 cup water
Serves: 1
Cooking technique: Blending
Steps: Peel the orange and grapefruit. Add the peeled fruits, honey, and water to the blender. Blend until smooth and refreshing.
Nutritional composition: Fat: 0.2g, Protein: 2g, Carbs: 28g, Fiber: 4g, Vitamin C, Natural Sugars
Calories: 120

Recipe 4: Spring Melon Medley

Prep time: 5 min
Components: 1 cup cantaloupe, 1 cup watermelon, 1 cup honeydew, 1 cup ice
Serves: 2
Cooking technique: Blending
Steps: Combine cantaloupe, watermelon, honeydew, and ice in the blender. Blend until you reach a slushy consistency.
Nutritional composition: Fat: 0.5g, Protein: 2g, Carbs: 22g, Fiber: 2g, Vitamin A, Vitamin C, Hydration

Calories: 90

Recipe 5: Protein Petal Punch

Prep time: 6 min
Components: 1 cup Greek yogurt, 1 tbsp pea protein powder, 1 cup strawberries, 1 tbsp honey
Serves: 1
Cooking technique: Blending
Steps: Add Greek yogurt, pea protein powder, strawberries, and honey to the blender. Blend to achieve a creamy perfection.
Nutritional composition: Fat: 1g, Protein: 28g, Carbs: 35g, Fiber: 4g, Calcium, Essential Amino Acids
Calories: 220

Recipe 6: Lavender Love Smoothie

Prep time: 8 min
Components: 1 cup almond milk, 1 tsp culinary lavender, 1 banana, 1 tsp honey
Serves: 1
Cooking technique: Blending
Steps: Combine almond milk, culinary lavender, banana, and honey in the blender. Blend until smooth; strain if preferred to remove lavender particles.
Nutritional composition: Fat: 3g, Protein: 2g, Carbs: 27g, Fiber: 3g, Potassium, Relaxing Properties

Calories: 170

Recipe 7: Minty Pineapple Paradise

Prep time: 5 min
Components: 1 cup pineapple, 5 fresh mint leaves, 1 cup coconut water
Serves: 1
Cooking technique: Blending
Steps: Place pineapple, fresh mint leaves, and coconut water in the blender. Blend until smooth and serve chilled.
Nutritional composition: Fat: 0.2g, Protein: 1g, Carbs: 25g, Fiber: 3g, Bromelain, Hydration
Calories: 140

Recipe 8: Choco-Banana Blossom

Prep time: 5
Components: 1 banana, 1 tbsp cacao powder, 1 cup almond milk
Serves: 1
Cooking technique: Blending
Steps: Add banana, cacao powder, and almond milk to the blender. Blend until you achieve a creamy, chocolaty consistency.
Nutritional composition: Fat: 3g, Protein: 3g, Carbs: 28g, Fiber: 6g, Potassium, Antioxidants
Calories: 200

Recipe 9: Floral Apricot Fusion

Prep time: 5 min
Components: 1 cup apricots, 1 tsp edible rose water, 1 cup yogurt
Serves: 1
Cooking technique: Blending
Steps: Place apricots, edible rose water, and yogurt in the blender. Blend until smooth.
Nutritional composition: Fat: 0.3g, Protein: 5g, Carbs: 29g, Fiber: 3g, Vitamin A, Calcium
Calories: 160

Recipe 10: Omega-Raspberry Elixir

Prep time: 5 min
Components: 1 cup raspberries, 1 tbsp flaxseeds, 1 cup oat milk
Serves: 1
Cooking technique: Blending
Steps: Combine raspberries, flaxseeds, and oat milk in the blender. Blend until smooth and serve immediately.
Nutritional composition: Fat: 9g, Protein: 3g, Carbs: 32g, Fiber: 8g, Omega-3s, Antioxidants, Vitamin C
Calories: 180

Summer Mornings:

Recipe 1: Tropical Sunshine Burst

Prep time: 5 min
Components: 1 cup mango chunks, 1 cup pineapple juice, 1 tsp coconut shavings
Serves: 1
Cooking technique: Blending
Steps: Blend mango chunks and pineapple juice until smooth. Garnish with coconut shavings and serve.
Nutritional composition: Fat: 0.5g, Protein: 1g, Carbs: 45g, Fiber: 3g, Vitamin C, Hydration
Calories: 180

Recipe 2: Peachy Keen Sunrise

Prep time: 6 min
Components: 2 ripe peaches, 1 cup almond milk, 1 tbsp agave nectar
Serves: 1
Cooking technique: Blending
Steps: Combine ripe peaches, almond milk, and agave nectar in the blender. Blend until creamy and smooth.
Nutritional composition: Fat: 2g, Protein: 3g, Carbs: 35g, Fiber: 3g, Vitamin A, Calcium
Calories: 160

Recipe 3: Zesty Lemon Quencher

Prep time: 5 min
Components: Juice of 2 lemons, 1 cup Greek yogurt, 1 tbsp honey
Serves: 1
Cooking technique: Blending

Steps: Add lemon juice, Greek yogurt, and honey to the blender. Blend to create a tangy, creamy mixture.
Nutritional composition: Fat: 0.2g, Protein: 15g, Carbs: 35g, Fiber: 0g, Vitamin C, Calcium
Calories: 200

Recipe 4: Kiwi Kale Kickstart

Prep time: 5 min
Components: 2 kiwis, 1 cup kale leaves, 1 cup coconut water
Serves: 1
Cooking technique: Blending
Steps: Place kiwis, kale leaves, and coconut water in the blender. Blend until smooth.
Nutritional composition: Fat: 1g, Protein: 3g, Carbs: 25g, Fiber: 5g, Vitamins A, C, K, Minerals
Calories: 120

Recipe 5: Cherry Almond Bliss

Prep time: 6 min
Components: 1 cup of pitted cherries, 1 cup almond milk, 1 tsp almond extract
Serves: 1
Cooking technique: Blending
Steps: Combine cherries, almond milk, and almond extract in the blender. Blend to achieve a smooth consistency.
Nutritional composition: Fat: 3g, Protein: 2g, Carbs: 25g, Fiber: 3g, Vitamin C, Calcium, Antioxidants
Calories: 180

Recipe 6: Blueberry Basil Boost

Prep time: 5 min
Components: 1 cup blueberries, 5 basil leaves, 1 cup soy milk
Serves: 1
Cooking technique: Blending
Steps: Add blueberries, basil leaves, and soy milk to the blender. Blend until the mixture is smooth and the basil is thoroughly mixed.
Nutritional composition: Fat: 2g, Protein: 7g, Carbs: 21g, Fiber: 4g, Vitamin C, Vitamin K, Antioxidants
Calories: 170

Recipe 7: Pomegranate Passion with seeds

Prep time: 7 min
Components: 1 cup pomegranate seeds, 1 banana, 1 cup water
Serves: 1
Cooking technique: Blending
Steps: Combine pomegranate seeds, banana, and water in the blender. Blend until velvety smooth.
Nutritional composition: Fat: 1g, Protein: 2g, Carbs: 35g, Fiber: 7g, Vitamin C, Fiber
Calories: 150

Recipe 8: Refreshing Watermelon Wave

Prep time: 4 min

Components: 2 cups watermelon, 1 tsp chia seeds

Serves: 2

Cooking technique: Blending

Steps: Blend watermelon until smooth. For a smoother texture, add chia seeds to the blender and blend until well combined; for added texture, stir chia seeds into the blended watermelon mixture after blending. Chill and serve.

Nutritional composition: Fat: 1g, Protein: 2g, Carbs: 22g, Fiber: 2g, Vitamin C, Omega-3s, Hydration

Calories: 100

Recipe 9: Spicy Mango Tango

Prep time: 6 min

Components: 1 cup mango, a pinch of cayenne pepper, 1 cup orange juice

Serves: 1

Cooking technique: Blending

Steps: Place mango chunks and ice in the blender; add orange juice to cover the fruit; sprinkle a pinch of cayenne pepper over the top. Blend on high until smooth, ensuring the cayenne pepper is fully incorporated

Nutritional composition: Fat: 0.5g, Protein: 2g, Carbs: 50g, Fiber: 3g, Vitamin A, Vitamin C

Calories: 200

Recipe 10: Creamy Cacao Cool-off

Prep time: 6 min

Components: 1 tbsp cacao nibs, 1 banana, 1 cup cashew milk

Serves: 1

Cooking technique: Blending

Steps: Add cacao nibs, banana, and cashew milk to the blender. Blend until creamy and smooth.

Nutritional composition: Fat: 4g, Protein: 4g, Carbs: 35g, Fiber: 7g, Potassium, Antioxidants

Calories: 220

Cozy Autumn

Recipe 1: Spiced Pumpkin Pleasure

Prep time: 5 min

Components: ½ cup pumpkin puree, 1 cup almond milk, 1 tsp pumpkin spice

Serves: 1

Cooking technique: Blending

Steps: Combine pumpkin puree, almond milk, and pumpkin spice in the blender. Blend until smooth.

Nutritional composition: Fat: 2g, Protein: 2g, Carbs: 30g, Fiber: 6g, Vitamin A, Fiber

Calories: 120

Recipe 2: Apple Pie Embrace

Prep time: 6 min
Components: 1 apple, 1 cup oat milk, 1 tsp cinnamon
Serves: 1
Cooking technique: Blending
Steps: Add apple, oat milk, and cinnamon to the blender. Blend until smooth, achieving an apple pie-like flavor.
Nutritional composition: Fat: 1g, Protein: 2g, Carbs: 28g, Fiber: 5g, Dietary Fiber, Vitamin C
Calories: 140

Recipe 3: Warm Ginger Zing

Prep time: 5 min
Components: 1 tsp ginger, 1 banana, 1 cup coconut milk
Serves: 1
Cooking technique: Blending
Steps: Add ginger, banana, and coconut milk to the blender. Blend to create a smooth, warming drink.
Nutritional composition: Fat: 5g, Protein: 2g, Carbs: 30g, Fiber: 3g, Immunity-boosting properties
Calories: 220

Recipe 4: Nutty Maple Hug

Prep time: 6 min
Components: 2 tbsp almond butter, 1 cup almond milk, 1 tbsp maple syrup
Serves: 1
Cooking technique: Blending
Steps: Combine almond butter, almond milk, and maple syrup in the blender. Blend until creamy and indulgent.
Nutritional composition: Fat: 15g, Protein: 8g, Carbs: 20g, Fiber: 3g, High in protein
Calories: 320

Recipe 5: Pear and Pecan Perfection

Prep time: 5 min
Components: 1 pear, 10 pecan halves, 1 cup water
Serves: 1
Cooking technique: Blending
Steps: Place the pear, pecan halves, and water into your blender and process until you achieve a creamy consistency.
Nutritional composition: Fat: 20g, Protein: 2g, Carbs: 28g, Fiber: 6g, Antioxidant-rich
Calories: 150

Recipe 6: Cranberry Crimson Crush

Prep time: 5 min
Components: 1 cup cranberries, 1 cup Greek yogurt, 1 tbsp honey
Serves: 1
Cooking technique: Blending

Steps: Combine the cranberries, Greek yogurt, and honey in your blender and blend until the texture is smooth.

Nutritional composition: Fat: 0.5g, Protein: 20g, Carbs: 35g, Fiber: 4g, Vitamin C, Protein

Calories: 190

Recipe 7: Sweet Potato Sunrise

Prep time: 7 min

Components: ½ cup sweet potato puree, 1 cup soy milk, 1 tsp cinnamon

Serves: 1

Cooking technique: Blending

Steps: Add sweet potato puree, soy milk, and cinnamon to your blender. Blend these ingredients thoroughly until the mixture is completely smooth.

Nutritional composition: Fat: 3g, Protein: 8g, Carbs: 30g, Fiber: 5g, Vitamin A, Fiber

Calories: 180

Recipe 8: Fig and Honey Harmony

Prep time: 6 min

Components: 4 figs, 1 cup Greek yogurt, 1 tbsp honey

Serves: 1

Cooking technique: Blending

Steps: Put the figs, Greek yogurt, and honey into your blender. Blend everything until smooth, resulting in a sweet and luxuriously creamy smoothie.

Nutritional composition: Fat: 0.5g, Protein: 15g, Carbs: 40g, Fiber: 5g, High in Fiber, Calcium

Calories: 210

Recipe 9: Chai Chilled Charm

Prep time: 5 min

Components: 1 cup chai tea (cooled), 1 banana, 1 cup oat milk

Serves: 1

Cooking technique: Blending

Steps: Brew a small cup of strong chai tea and let it cool. In the blender, combine the cooled chai tea, banana, and oat milk. Blend until the mixture is smooth.

Nutritional composition: Fat: 2g, Protein: 4g, Carbs: 30g, Fiber: 4g, Antioxidants

Calories: 170

Recipe 10: Caramel Apple Crave

Prep time: 6 min

Components: 1 apple, 1 cup almond milk, 1 tbsp caramel extract

Serves: 1

Cooking technique: Blending

Steps: Add an apple, almond milk, and caramel extract to your blender. Blend until the mixture reaches a smooth, dessert-like consistency.

Nutritional composition: Fat: 1g, Protein: 2g, Carbs: 30g, Fiber: 4g, Fiber-rich

Calories: 200

Winter Energy

Recipe 1: Winterberry Warmth

Prep time: 5 min

Components: 1 cup mixed berries (blueberries, raspberries, blackberries), 1 cup warm chamomile tea, 1 tbsp honey

Serves: 1

Cooking technique: Blending

Steps: Combine mixed berries, warm chamomile tea, and honey in your blender. Process until smooth to enjoy a warming and soothing blend.

Nutritional composition: Fat: 0.5g, Protein: 1g, Carbs: 30g, Fiber: 6g, Antioxidants, Soothing properties

Calories: 120

Recipe 2: Mocha Motivator

Prep time: 6 min

Components: 1 cup cold brew coffee, 1 banana, 1 tbsp cocoa powder

Serves: 1

Cooking technique: Blending

Steps: Start with cold brew coffee as the base and pour it into the blender. Add a scoop of chocolate protein powder for a mocha flavor. Throw in a handful of ice cubes. Blend until you achieve a smooth consistency.

Nutritional composition: Fat: 1g, Protein: 2g, Carbs: 30g, Fiber: 3g, Energy-boosting, Caffeine

Calories: 150

Recipe 3: Peppermint Pep

Prep time: 5 min

Components: 1 cup almond milk, 1 tbsp peppermint extract, 1 tbsp chia seeds

Serves: 1

Cooking technique: Blending

Steps: Add fresh peppermint leaves and spinach to the blender for a green base. Include slices of green apple and banana for natural sweetness. Pour in a bit of water or ice for desired thickness. Blend everything until smooth.

Nutritional composition: Fat: 4g, Protein: 3g, Carbs: 15g, Fiber: 5g, Omega-3s, Refreshing properties

Calories: 160

Recipe 4: Spicy Ginger Glow

Prep time: 5 min

Components: 1 tsp ginger, 1 apple, 1 cup water

Serves: 1
Cooking technique: Blending
Steps: Peel and slice fresh ginger root and add to the blender. Incorporate carrot juice and frozen peaches for sweetness and body. Add a squeeze of lemon juice for acidity. Blend on high until completely smooth.
Nutritional composition: Fat: 0.2g, Protein: 1g, Carbs: 22g, Fiber: 4g, Antioxidants, Digestive health
Calories: 100

Recipe 5: Power Matcha Mix

Prep time: 5 min
Components: 1 tsp matcha powder, 1 banana, 1 cup soy milk
Serves: 1
Cooking technique: Blending
Steps: Combine matcha powder, banana, and soy milk in the blender. Blend to a smooth, energetic consistency.
Nutritional composition: Fat: 2g, Protein: 8g, Carbs: 25g, Fiber: 3g, Antioxidants, Energy-boosting
Calories: 200

Recipe 6: Cocoa Comfort

Prep time: 6 min
Components: 1 tbsp cocoa, 1 cup oat milk, 1 tbsp almond butter
Serves: 1
Cooking technique: Blending
Steps: Add cocoa, oat milk, and almond butter to the blender. Blend for a creamy and comforting start.
Nutritional composition: Fat: 15g, Protein: 5g, Carbs: 20g, Fiber: 4g, High in protein, Comforting
Calories: 250

Recipe 7: Energizing Beet Boost

Prep time: 7 min
Components: ½ beetroot, 1 apple, 1 cup water
Serves: 1
Cooking technique: Blending
Steps: Add beetroot, apple, and water to your blender. Blend until smooth for a naturally sweet and energizing smoothie.
Nutritional composition: Fat: 0.2g, Protein: 2g, Carbs: 25g, Fiber: 6g, Nitrates, Energy-boosting
Calories: 140

Recipe 8: Nutmeg Nectar

Prep time: 5 min
Components: 1 pear, 1 cup Greek yogurt, 1 tsp nutmeg
Serves: 1
Cooking technique: Blending

Steps: Wash, peel, and core the pear, then cut it into chunks. Add the pear chunks to the blender with Greek yogurt and nutmeg. Blend until the mixture is creamy and smooth, ensuring the nutmeg is thoroughly incorporated.

Nutritional composition: Fat: 1g, Protein: 15g, Carbs: 30g, Fiber: 4g, High in calcium, Digestive health

Calories: 180

Recipe 9: Guarana Gusto

Prep time: 5 min

Components: 1 tsp guarana powder, 1 banana, 1 cup coconut milk

Serves: 1

Cooking technique: Blending

Steps: Add guarana powder, banana, and coconut milk to the blender. Blend until you achieve a smooth consistency, ensuring the guarana powder is fully incorporated.

.**Nutritional composition:** Fat: 5g, Protein: 2g, Carbs: 35g, Fiber: 3g, Energy and potassium-rich, Caffeine

Calories: 220

Recipe 10: Raspberry Revival

Prep time: 5 min

Components: 1 cup raspberries, 1 cup almond milk, 1 tbsp flaxseeds

Serves: 1

Cooking technique: Blending

Steps: Into the blender, add raspberries, almond milk, and flaxseeds. Blend until the texture is smooth and the flaxseeds are fully integrated.

Nutritional composition: Fat: 9g, Protein: 4g, Carbs: 23g, Fiber: 9g, Omega-3s, Vitamin C, Antioxidants

Calories: 180

CHAPTER 2: Lunchtime Smoothie Recipes

Spring Greens

Recipe 1: Verdant Zest

Prep time: 5 min
Components: 1 cup spinach, 1/2 avocado, 1/2 cup green grapes, 1/2 cup coconut water, zest of 1 lemon
Serves: 1
Cooking technique: Blending
Steps: Combine spinach, avocado, grapes, and coconut water in a blender. Add lemon zest and blend until smooth.
Nutritional composition: Fat: 7g, Protein: 2g, Carbs: 22g, Fiber: 5g, Vitamins A, C, E, Healthy Fats
Calories: 220

Recipe 2: Herbal Harmony

Prep time: 5 min
Components: 1 cup kale, handful of fresh mint, 1/2 cup pineapple chunks, 1 cup almond milk
Serves: 1
Cooking technique: Blending
Steps: Place kale, mint, pineapple, and almond milk into the blender. Blend until creamy and smooth.
Nutritional composition: Fat: 1g, Protein: 3g, Carbs: 20g, Fiber: 3g, Vitamin K, Antioxidants
Calories: 190

Recipe 3: Green Zen

Prep time: 6 min
Components: 1 cup matcha tea, 1/2 cucumber, 1 tbsp chia seeds, 1 tsp agave nectar
Serves: 1
Cooking technique: Blending
Steps: Pour matcha tea into the blender, add sliced cucumber, chia seeds, and agave nectar. Blend all the ingredients until the mixture is uniformly smooth, ensuring a creamy texture with fully incorporated chia seeds.
Nutritional composition: Fat: 4g, Protein: 3g, Carbs: 17g, Fiber: 5g, Omega-3, Antioxidants, Energy-Boosting
Calories: 160

Recipe 4: Spring Sprout

Prep time: 5 min
Components: 1 cup broccoli sprouts, 1 green apple, 1 cup water, 1 tbsp flaxseeds
Serves: 1
Cooking technique: Blending

Steps: Combine broccoli sprouts, cored and sliced green apple, water, and flaxseeds in the blender. Blend everything together until the mixture is completely smooth, ensuring the flaxseeds are well integrated and the texture is even.

Nutritional composition: Fat: 4g, Protein: 3g, Carbs: 24g, Fiber: 7g, Sulforaphane, Fiber

Calories: 140

Recipe 5: Asparagus Ascend

Prep time: 7 min

Components: 5 asparagus spears, 1/2 cup arugula, 1 cup coconut milk, 1 tsp honey

Serves: 1

Cooking technique: Blending

Steps: Trim and chop the asparagus spears, then place them in the blender along with arugula, coconut milk, and honey. Blend until the mixture is smooth, ensuring the asparagus and arugula are thoroughly pureed for a creamy consistency.

Nutritional composition: Fat: 5g, Protein: 3g, Carbs: 10g, Fiber: 3g, Folate, Vitamin K

Calories: 200

Recipe 6: Celery Citrus Sip

Prep time: 5 min

Components: 2 celery stalks, 1/2 grapefruit, 1 cup water

Serves: 1

Cooking technique: Blending

Steps: Place chopped celery stalks and half a grapefruit into the blender with a cup of water. Blend until the texture is smooth and the flavors are well combined.

Nutritional composition: Fat: 0.2g, Protein: 1g, Carbs: 18g, Fiber: 3g, Vitamins, Hydration

Calories: 90

Recipe 7: Pea & Mint Magic

Prep time: 5 min

Components: 1 cup fresh peas, handful of mint leaves, 1 cup oat milk

Serves: 1

Cooking technique: Blending

Steps: Add fresh peas, a handful of mint leaves, and oat milk to the blender. Process until the mixture is smooth, ensuring the mint is finely blended with the peas.

Nutritional composition: Fat: 2g, Protein: 5g, Carbs: 25g, Fiber: 6g, Protein, Fiber, Freshness

Calories: 180

Recipe 8: Watercress Wonder

Prep time: 5 min

Components: 1 cup watercress, 1/2 cup Greek yogurt, 1 pear, 1 tbsp honey

Serves: 1

Cooking technique: Blending

Steps: Combine watercress, Greek yogurt, chopped pear, and honey in the blender. Blend until the mixture is smooth, making sure the pear is completely pureed and the yogurt is fully integrated with the greens.
Nutritional composition: Fat: 1g, Protein: 10g, Carbs: 26g, Fiber: 4g, Vitamin A, Vitamin C, Probiotics
Calories: 210

Recipe 9: Spring Basil Bliss

Prep time: 5 min
Components: Handful of basil leaves, 1 cup spinach, 1/2 lemon juice, 1 cup water
Serves: 1
Cooking technique: Blending
Steps: Add a handful of basil leaves, spinach, lemon juice, and water to the blender. Blend until the mixture is smooth, ensuring that the basil and spinach are thoroughly incorporated into a revitalizing drink.
Nutritional composition: Fat: 0.3g, Protein: 2g, Carbs: 7g, Fiber: 2g, Vitamin C, Iron, Refreshing Flavors
Calories: 60

Summertime Joy

Recipe 1: Berry Bliss Burst

Prep time: 5 min
Components: 1 cup mixed berries (blueberries, raspberries, strawberries), 1 cup coconut water, 1 tbsp chia seeds
Serves: 1
Cooking technique: Blending
Steps: Place mixed berries, coconut water, and chia seeds into the blender. Blend until the berries are completely pureed and the chia seeds are well mixed into a smooth and delicious smoothie.
Nutritional composition: Fat: 3g, Protein: 2g, Carbs: 30g, Fiber: 8g, Antioxidants, Omega-3 Fatty Acids
Calories: 150

Recipe 2: Mango Melody

Prep time: 6 min
Components: 1 ripe mango, 1/2 cup Greek yogurt, 1 tbsp honey, 1 cup ice
Serves: 1
Cooking technique: Blending
Steps: Peel and slice mango. Blend mango, Greek yogurt, honey, and ice until achieving a creamy texture.
Nutritional composition: Fat: 0.5g, Protein: 8g, Carbs: 55g, Fiber: 3g, Vitamins A, C, Probiotics
Calories: 210

Recipe 3: Sunlit Citrus Splash

Prep time: 5 min

Components: 1 orange, 1/2 cup pineapple chunks, 1 cup almond milk
Serves: 1
Cooking technique: Blending
Steps: Peel the orange and blend with pineapple chunks and almond milk for a smooth, refreshing drink.
Nutritional composition: Fat: 2g, Protein: 2g, Carbs: 29g, Fiber: 4g, Vitamin C, Calcium
Calories: 180

Recipe 4: Kiwi & Kale Dance

Prep time: 5 min
Components: 2 kiwis, 1 cup kale, 1 cup water, 1 tsp spirulina powder
Serves: 1
Cooking technique: Blending
Steps: Peel kiwis and blend with kale, water, and spirulina powder until smooth.
Nutritional composition: Fat: 1g, Protein: 5g, Carbs: 21g, Fiber: 5g, Vitamin K, Antioxidants
Calories: 130

Recipe 5: Minty Watermelon Wave

Prep time: 5 min
Components: 2 cups watermelon cubes, handful of mint leaves, juice of 1 lime
Serves: 1-2
Cooking technique: Blending
Steps: Combine watermelon cubes with mint leaves and freshly squeezed lime juice in the blender. Process everything until you achieve a hydrating and invigorating smoothie, perfect for cooling off on a hot day.
Nutritional composition: Fat: 0.5g, Protein: 2g, Carbs: 22g, Fiber: 1g, Hydration, Vitamins
Calories: 100

Recipe 6: Passionfruit Paradise

Prep time: 7 min
Components: Pulp of 2 passionfruits, 1 cup yogurt, 1 tbsp agave nectar
Serves: 1
Cooking technique: Blending
Steps: Scoop the pulp from two passionfruits into the blender, adding yogurt and agave nectar. Blend all the ingredients until the mixture becomes a richly flavored, tropical smoothie.
Nutritional composition: Fat: 1g, Protein: 8g, Carbs: 36g, Fiber: 10g, Vitamin A, C, Probiotics
Calories: 190

Recipe 7: Cool Cucumber Melange

Prep time: 5 min
Components: 1 cucumber, 1/2 lemon juice, 1 cup cold water

Serves: 1
Cooking technique: Blending
Steps: Add sliced cucumber, freshly squeezed lemon juice, and cold water to the blender. Blend until the mixture is exceptionally smooth, creating a super-refreshing beverage ideal for replenishing hydration.
Nutritional composition: Fat: 0.2g, Protein: 2g, Carbs: 11g, Fiber: 2g, Hydration, Vitamin C
Calories: 50

Recipe 8: Papaya Peach Fusion

Prep time: 6 min
Components: 1 cup papaya, 1 peach, 1 cup soy milk
Serves: 1
Cooking technique: Blending
Steps: Place chopped papaya, peach slices, and soy milk into the blender. Blend until the mixture is smooth, offering a creamy and nutritious smoothie that marries the flavors of papaya and peach beautifully.
Nutritional composition: Fat: 2g, Protein: 6g, Carbs: 28g, Fiber: 4g, Vitamin C, A, Isoflavones
Calories: 170

Recipe 9: Zesty Cherry Chill

Prep time: 5 min
Components: 1 cup of pitted cherries, 1/2 lime juice, 1 cup coconut milk
Serves: 1
Cooking technique: Blending
Steps: Put cherries, lime juice, and coconut milk in the blender. Blend until smooth to craft a zesty and creamy drink that combines the tangy sharpness of lime with the sweet depth of cherries.
Nutritional composition: Fat: 4g, Protein: 2g, Carbs: 22g, Fiber: 3g, Antioxidants, Vitamin C
Calories: 200

Autumn Harvest

Recipe 1: Autumn Maple Melody

Prep time: 6 min
Components: 1 cup roasted acorn squash, 2 tbsp pure maple syrup, 1 cup almond milk
Serves: 1
Cooking technique: Blending
Steps: Ensure the acorn squash is roasted beforehand to save time. (To roast acorn squash: Preheat your oven to 400°F (200°C). Cut the squash in half and scoop out the seeds. Place the halves cut side up on a baking sheet and roast until the flesh is tender, about 30-35 minutes).

To prepare the smoothie, simply scoop out a cup of the roasted squash flesh into a blender, add maple syrup and almond milk, and blend until smooth.

Nutritional composition: Fat: 1.5g, Protein: 2g, Carbs: 37g, Fiber: 6g, Vitamin A, Minerals

Calories: 180

Recipe 2: Apple Orchard Delight

Prep time: 5 min

Components: 2 apples, 1 cup Greek yogurt, 1 tsp cinnamon

Serves: 1

Cooking technique: Blending

Steps: Core and chop apples, then blend them with Greek yogurt and a sprinkle of cinnamon. Blend until smooth.

Nutritional composition: Fat: 0.5g, Protein: 10g, Carbs: 36g, Fiber: 5g, Probiotics, Vitamins

Calories: 200

Recipe 3: Cranberry Crush

Prep time: 6 min

Components: 1 cup cranberries, 1 banana, 1 cup oat milk

Serves: 1

Cooking technique: Blending

Steps: Place cranberries and a peeled banana into the blender, add oat milk, and blend until the smoothie is smooth and well-combined.

Nutritional composition: Fat: 1.5g, Protein: 2g, Carbs: 40g, Fiber: 7g, Antioxidants, Potassium

Calories: 180

Recipe 4: Fig & Date Symphony

Prep time: 7 min

Components: 4 figs, 2 dates, 1 cup soy milk

Serves: 1

Cooking technique: Blending

Steps: Put figs and dates into the blender, add soy milk, and blend until the mixture becomes creamy and smooth.

Nutritional composition: Fat: 1g, Protein: 6g, Carbs: 58g, Fiber: 10g, Fiber, Calcium

Calories: 220

Recipe 5: Nutty Butternut Bliss

Prep time: 10 min

Components: 1 cup butternut squash (cooked), 1 tbsp almond butter, 1 cup cashew milk

Serves: 1

Cooking technique: Blending

Steps: Place cooked butternut squash in the blender, add almond butter and cashew milk, and blend until the texture is velvety and consistent.

Nutritional composition: Fat: 9g, Protein: 4g, Carbs: 36g, Fiber: 6g, Vitamin A, Healthy Fats

Calories: 230

Recipe 6: Pecan Pie Smoothie

Prep time: 6 min

Components: 1 cup pecans, 1 tsp maple syrup, 1 cup vanilla yogurt

Serves: 1

Cooking technique: Blending

Steps: Add pecans, maple syrup, and vanilla yogurt to the blender. Blend until the mixture is smooth and mimics the flavors of a pecan pie.

Nutritional composition: Fat: 20g, Protein: 8g, Carbs: 30g, Fiber: 4g, Healthy Fats, Probiotics

Calories: 310

Recipe 7: Golden Persimmon Potion

Prep time: 5 min

Components: 2 persimmons, 1 cup coconut water

Serves: 1

Cooking technique: Blending

Steps: Slice persimmons, place them in the blender, add coconut water, and blend until the smoothie is smooth, capturing the fresh taste of persimmons.

Nutritional composition: Fat: 0.3g, Protein: 1g, Carbs: 38g, Fiber: 6g, Vitamins A, C

Calories: 150

Recipe 8: Sweet Potato Euphoria

Prep time: 10 min

Components: 1 cup sweet potato (cooked), 1 tsp honey, 1 cup almond milk

Serves: 1

Cooking technique: Blending

Steps: Ensure the sweet potato is cooked beforehand. Add the cooked sweet potato, honey, and almond milk to the blender. Blend until the mixture is smooth, creating a creamy, flavorful smoothie.

Nutritional composition: Fat: 1.5g, Protein: 2g, Carbs: 40g, Fiber: 6g, Vitamin A, Fiber

Calories: 200

Recipe 9: Chai-infused Pear Perfection

Prep time: 6 min

Components: 2 pears, 1 tsp chai spice, 1 cup oat milk

Serves: 1

Cooking technique: Blending

Steps: Chop the pears and add them to the blender along with chai spice and oat milk. Blend until smooth, allowing the chai to infuse throughout the smoothie.

Nutritional composition: Fat: 1g, Protein: 2g, Carbs: 42g, Fiber: 8g, Fiber, Spices

Calories: 170

Winter Wellness

Recipe 1: Immunity Boosting Blend

Prep time: 5 mins

Components: 1 cup kale, 1/2 cup blueberries, 1 tsp chia seeds, 1 tbsp manuka honey, 1 cup almond milk

Serves: 1

Cooking technique: Blending

Steps: Combine kale, blueberries, chia seeds, manuka honey, and almond milk in the blender. Blend until the mixture is completely smooth, ensuring the chia seeds are fully integrated.

Nutritional composition: Fat: 4g, Protein: 3g, Carbs: 28g, Fiber: 6g, High in antioxidants, Vitamins C and K

Calories: 180

Recipe 2: Creamy Cacao Comfort

Prep time: 7 mins

Components: 2 tbsp raw cacao nibs, 1 cup oat milk, 1 banana, 1 tbsp almond butter

Serves: 1

Cooking technique: Blending

Steps: Add raw cacao nibs, oat milk, a banana, and almond butter into the blender. Blend everything until it achieves a uniformly creamy texture, making sure the cacao nibs are thoroughly incorporated.

Nutritional composition: Fat: 15g, Protein: 6g, Carbs: 30g, Fiber: 6g, Rich in magnesium and fiber

Calories: 250

Recipe 3: Spicy Turmeric Tango

Prep time: 5 mins

Components: 1 cup coconut milk, 1 tsp turmeric, 1/2 tsp cinnamon, pinch of black pepper, 1 tbsp agave nectar

Serves: 1

Cooking technique: Blending

Steps: Pour coconut milk into the blender and add turmeric, cinnamon, a pinch of black pepper, and agave nectar. Blend all the ingredients until the mixture is smooth and the spices are well mixed.

Nutritional composition: Fat: 12g, Protein: 2g, Carbs: 15g, Fiber: 1g, Anti-inflammatory properties

Calories: 210

Recipe 4: Gingered Pear Perfection

Prep time: 6 mins

Components: 2 ripe pears, 1 tsp fresh ginger, 1 cup Greek yogurt, 1 tsp flaxseeds

Serves: 1

Cooking technique: Blending

Steps: Begin by peeling and coring the ripe pears. Add them to a blender along with the peeled fresh ginger, Greek yogurt, and flaxseeds. Blend the mixture until it reaches a smooth, uniform consistency.

Nutritional composition: Fat: 2g, Protein: 8g, Carbs: 27g, Fiber: 6g, Rich in dietary fiber, probiotics, Vitamin C, and the digestive benefits of ginger.

Calories: 220

Recipe 5: Energizing Espresso Elixir

Prep time: 5 mins

Components: 1 shot espresso, 1 cup soy milk, 1 tbsp chia seeds, 1 tbsp maple syrup

Serves: 1

Cooking technique: Blending

Steps: Start by adding a shot of espresso to the blender, followed by soy milk, chia seeds, and maple syrup. Blend until smooth, ensuring the chia seeds are fully broken down and mixed.

Nutritional composition: Fat: 4g, Protein: 8g, Carbs: 22g, Fiber: 6g, Source of caffeine and omega-3 fatty acids

Calories: 180

Recipe 6: Walnut Wonder with kefir

Prep time: 7 mins

Components: 1 cup walnuts, 1/2 cup pomegranate seeds, 1 cup kefir, 1 tbsp honey

Serves: 1

Cooking technique: Blending

Steps: Place walnuts, pomegranate seeds, kefir, and honey in the blender. Blend until the mixture reaches a smooth consistency, ensuring the walnuts and pomegranate seeds are completely pureed.

Nutritional composition: Fat: 19g, Protein: 9g, Carbs: 20g, Fiber: 4g, High in omega-3 fatty acids and antioxidants

Calories: 320

Recipe 7: Berry Citrus Symphony

Prep time: 6 mins

Components: 1/2 cup cranberries, 1 orange (peeled), 1 cup Greek yogurt, 1 tsp honey

Serves: 1

Cooking technique: Blending

Steps: Add cranberries, a peeled orange, Greek yogurt, and honey to the blender. Blend until the mixture becomes creamy and smooth, ensuring the orange is fully incorporated without any chunks.

Nutritional composition: Fat: 1g, Protein: 10g, Carbs: 35g, Fiber: 4g, High in Vitamin C and probiotics
Calories: 200

Recipe 8: Chilly Chaga Charm

Prep time: 5 mins
Components: 1 tsp chaga mushroom powder, 1 cup almond milk, 1 banana, 1 tbsp honey
Serves: 1
Cooking technique: Blending
Steps: Combine chaga mushroom powder, almond milk, a banana, and honey in a blender. Blend until the mixture is smooth and the mushroom powder is completely dissolved.
Nutritional composition: Fat: 3g, Protein: 2g, Carbs: 30g, Fiber: 4g, Immune-boosting properties
Calories: 190

Recipe 9: Avocado Almond Ambrosia

Prep time: 7 mins
Components: 1 avocado, 1 cup almond milk, 1 tsp vanilla extract, 1 tbsp agave syrup
Serves: 1
Cooking technique: Blending
Steps: Cut the avocado and remove the pit. Add the avocado flesh to the blender along with almond milk, vanilla extract, and agave syrup. Blend until the mixture is smooth and creamy, with all ingredients fully combined.
Nutritional composition: Fat: 15g, Protein: 3g, Carbs: 25g, Fiber: 7g, Rich in healthy fats and vitamins
Calories: 250

CHAPTER 3: Dinner Smoothie Recipes

Spring Detox

Recipe 1: Green Machine Medley

Prep time: 5 mins
Components: 1 cup spinach, 1/2 cucumber, 1 apple, 1 tbsp spirulina, 1 cup coconut water
Serves: 1
Cooking technique: Blending
Steps: Roughly chop fresh spinach, cucumber, and apple. Add these along with spirulina and coconut water to a blender. Blend until the mixture is smooth and homogenous.
Nutritional composition: Fat: 1g, Protein: 2g, Carbs: 25g, Fiber: 5g, Rich in chlorophyll, vitamins A, C, E, and essential minerals.
Calories: 160

Recipe 2: Fresh Mint Mirage

Prep time: 7 mins
Components: 10 fresh mint leaves, 1 kiwi, 1/2 lemon (juiced), 1 tsp chlorella powder, 1 cup water
Serves: 1
Cooking technique: Blending
Steps: Combine the mint leaves, peeled and sliced kiwi, lemon juice, chlorella powder, and water in a blender. Blend until smooth to enjoy a refreshing and detoxifying drink.
Nutritional composition: Fat: 0.5g, Protein: 2g, Carbs: 20g, Fiber: 4g, High in vitamin K, antioxidants, and detoxifying properties.
Calories: 120

Recipe 3: Celery Serenity

Prep time: 6 mins
Components: 3 celery stalks, 1/2 green apple, 1/2 lime (juiced), 1 inch ginger root, 1 cup almond milk
Serves: 1
Cooking technique: Blending
Steps: Chop celery and apple, and grate the ginger. Add these ingredients to a blender with lime juice and almond milk. Blend until you achieve a serene, smooth mixture.
Nutritional composition: Fat: 1.5g, Protein: 1g, Carbs: 15g, Fiber: 3g, Rich in vitamins A, K, anti-inflammatory properties.
Calories: 140

Recipe 4: Dandelion Delight

Prep time: 5 mins
Components: 1 cup dandelion greens, 1 pear, 1 tsp MSM powder, 1 cup green tea (cooled)

Serves: 1

Cooking technique: Blending

Steps: Blend the dandelion greens, cored and sliced pear, MSM powder, and cooled green tea until it forms a delightful smooth drink.

Nutritional composition: Fat: 0.5g, Protein: 1g, Carbs: 25g, Fiber: 4g, High in calcium, liver detoxification properties.

Calories: 110

Recipe 5: Pineapple Paradise

Prep time: 7 mins

Components: 1/2 cup pineapple, 1/2 tsp activated charcoal, 1 cup chamomile tea (cooled)

Serves: 1

Cooking technique: Blending

Steps: Add fresh or canned pineapple chunks, activated charcoal, and cooled chamomile tea to a blender and mix until it reaches a paradise-like smoothness.

Nutritional composition: Fat: 0.2g, Protein: 1g, Carbs: 20g, Fiber: 2g, Bromelain for digestion, relaxation properties from chamomile.

Calories: 150

Recipe 6: Fennel Fusion

Prep time: 5 mins

Components: 1/2 bulb fennel, 1 orange, 1 tbsp flaxseeds, 1 cup water

Serves: 1

Cooking technique: Blending

Steps: Chop the fennel and orange, then blend them with flaxseeds and water for a uniquely combined smoothie.

Nutritional composition: Fat: 4g, Protein: 2g, Carbs: 27g, Fiber: 7g, Rich in Vitamin C, fiber, and omega-3 fatty acids.

Calories: 180

Recipe 7: Beetroot Bliss

Prep time: 7 mins

Components: 1 small beetroot, 1/2 apple, 1 carrot, 1 tsp maca powder, 1 cup oat milk

Serves: 1

Cooking technique: Blending

Steps: Peel and roughly chop the beetroot, apple, and carrot. Place them into the blender with maca powder and oat milk. Blend until the mixture is completely smooth, ensuring there are no chunks left for a creamy texture.

Nutritional composition: Fat: 1g, Protein: 3g, Carbs: 28g, Fiber: 6g, High in nitrates, energy-boosting.

Calories: 190

Recipe 8: Radiant Raspberry

Prep time: 5 mins

Components: 1/2 cup raspberries, 1 tbsp goji berries, 1 tbsp chia seeds, 1 cup rooibos tea (cooled)

Serves: 1
Cooking technique: Blending
Steps: Place raspberries, goji berries, chia seeds, and cooled rooibos tea into the blender. Blend until the mixture is smooth, ensuring the seeds and berries are fully incorporated into a vibrant smoothie.
Nutritional composition: Fat: 2g, Protein: 3g, Carbs: 20g, Fiber: 5g, Antioxidants, omega-3.
Calories: 160

Recipe 9: Lemon Lush

Prep time: 5 mins
Components: 1 lemon (peeled), 1 tbsp honey, 1 tbsp hemp seeds, 1 cup water
Serves: 1
Cooking technique: Blending
Steps: Add the peeled lemon, honey, hemp seeds, and water into the blender. Blend until the mixture is thoroughly combined and smooth, creating a tangy and refreshing drink.
Nutritional composition: Fat: 3g, Protein: 4g, Carbs: 20g, Fiber: 3g, Vitamin C, omega-3, and omega-6.
Calories: 140

Recipe 10: Turmeric Twist

Prep time: 6 mins
Components: 1/2 tsp turmeric, 1/2 tsp black pepper, 1 tbsp coconut oil, 1 cup coconut milk
Serves: 1
Cooking technique: Blending
Steps: Combine turmeric, black pepper, coconut oil, and coconut milk in the blender. Blend until the mixture is smooth and uniform, ensuring the coconut oil is completely emulsified into the smoothie.
Nutritional composition: Fat: 14g, Protein: 2g, Carbs: 6g, Fiber: 1g, Anti-inflammatory, healthy fats.
Calories: 200

Summer Sunset

Recipe 1: Tropical Harmony

Prep time: 5 mins
Components: 1 cup mango, 1 passionfruit, 1 tbsp baobab powder, 1 cup coconut water
Serves: 1
Cooking technique: Blending
Steps: Add mango chunks, the pulp of one passionfruit, baobab powder, and coconut water to the blender. Blend until smooth and homogenous, ensuring all ingredients are well combined for a tropical-flavored smoothie.
Nutritional composition: Fat: 0.5g, Protein: 2g, Carbs: 30g, Fiber: 5g, Rich in vitamin C and antioxidants.

Calories: 170

Recipe 2: Berry Bliss with Acai

Prep time: 6 mins

Components: 1/2 cup strawberries, 1/2 cup blueberries, 1 tbsp acai powder, 1 cup almond milk

Serves: 1

Cooking technique: Blending

Steps: Add strawberries, blueberries, acai powder, and almond milk to the blender. Blend until the consistency is smooth and creamy, ensuring the berries are fully pureed.

Nutritional composition: Fat: 1g, Protein: 2g, Carbs: 25g, Fiber: 6g, Antioxidants, vitamin K.

Calories: 160

Recipe 3: Peachy Serenity

Prep time: 5 mins

Components: 1 peach, 1/2 banana, 1 tbsp camu camu powder, 1 cup cold green tea

Serves: 1

Cooking technique: Blending

Steps: Slice the peach and banana, add them to the blender along with camu camu powder and cold green tea. Blend everything together until the mixture is smooth.

Nutritional composition: Fat: 0.3g, Protein: 1g, Carbs: 28g, Fiber: 3g, Vitamin C, antioxidants.

Calories: 140

Recipe 4: Citrus Glow

Prep time: 7 mins

Components: 1/2 grapefruit, 1 orange, 1 tsp bee pollen, 1 cup water

Serves: 1

Cooking technique: Blending

Steps: Peel and segment the grapefruit and orange, combine them in the blender with bee pollen and water. Blend until the mixture is smooth.

Nutritional composition: Fat: 0.2g, Protein: 2g, Carbs: 26g, Fiber: 3g, Vitamin C, bioflavonoids.

Calories: 130

Recipe 5: Cherry Charm with Goji

Prep time: 5 mins

Components: 1 cup cherries, 1/2 pomegranate, 1 tbsp goji berries, 1 cup cashew milk

Serves: 1

Cooking technique: Blending

Steps: Pit the cherries and extract seeds from the pomegranate. Add these with goji berries and cashew milk to the blender. Blend until the smoothie is smooth, ensuring all components are well combined.

Nutritional composition: Fat: 1.5g, Protein: 3g, Carbs: 30g, Fiber: 5g, Antioxidants, vitamin A.

Calories: 180

Recipe 6: Watermelon Whisper

Prep time: 7 mins
Components: 1 cup watermelon, 1 tbsp rose petals, 1 tsp lucuma powder, 1 cup water
Serves: 1
Cooking technique: Blending
Steps: Cube fresh, chilled watermelon and add it to the blender with rose petals, lucuma powder, and water. Blend until you achieve a light, hydrating smoothie perfect for quenching thirst.
Nutritional composition: Fat: 0.2g, Protein: 1g, Carbs: 20g, Fiber: 1g, Hydration, vitamin A.
Calories: 120

Recipe 7: Sunset Serenade

Prep time: 6 mins
Components: 1/2 papaya, 1/2 cup pineapple, 1 tsp ashwagandha powder, 1 cup coconut milk
Serves: 1
Cooking technique: Blending
Steps: Chop the papaya and pineapple, and add them to the blender along with ashwagandha powder and coconut milk. Blend until the mixture is perfectly smooth.
Nutritional composition: Fat: 3g, Protein: 2g, Carbs: 30g, Fiber: 5g, Digestive enzymes, adaptogens.

Calories: 200

Recipe 8: Apricot Euphoria

Prep time: 5 mins
Components: 2 apricots, 1 tbsp almond butter, 1 tsp maqui berry powder, 1 cup soy milk
Serves: 1
Cooking technique: Blending
Steps: Halve and pit the apricots, then add them to the blender with almond butter, maqui berry powder, and soy milk. Blend until smooth, making sure the apricots are thoroughly pureed into the mix.
Nutritional composition: Fat: 4g, Protein: 6g, Carbs: 20g, Fiber: 3g, Vitamin A, protein.
Calories: 180

Recipe 9: Plum Passion

Prep time: 7 mins
Components: 2 plums, 1/2 cup blackberries, 1 tbsp chia seeds, 1 cup oat milk
Serves: 1
Cooking technique: Blending
Steps: Pit and quarter the plums, add them to the blender with blackberries, chia seeds, and oat milk. Blend until smooth, ensuring the seeds and skin are fully integrated into the smoothie for maximum fiber.

Nutritional composition: Fat: 3g, Protein: 4g, Carbs: 35g, Fiber: 7g, Fiber, omega-3.
Calories: 150

Recipe 10: Guava Grace

Prep time: 5 mins
Components: 1 guava, 1 tbsp honey, 1 tsp moringa powder, 1 cup rice milk
Serves: 1
Cooking technique: Blending
Steps: Slice the guava, removing any seeds, and add it to the blender with honey, moringa powder, and rice milk. Blend until the texture is smooth and velvety.
Nutritional composition: Fat: 1g, Protein: 2g, Carbs: 25g, Fiber: 5g, Vitamin C, iron.
Calories: 170

Fall Comfort

Recipe 1: Cinnamon Apple Crisp

Prep time: 5 mins
Components: 1 apple, 1 cup almond milk, 1 tsp cinnamon, 1 tbsp honey
Serves: 1
Cooking technique: Blending
Steps: Core and chop the apple, then place it in a blender with almond milk, cinnamon, and honey. Blend until the mixture is completely smooth.

Nutritional composition: Fat: 1g, Protein: 1g, Carbs: 28g, Fiber: 4g, Vitamin C, Antioxidants.
Calories: 150

Recipe 2: Cozy Pumpkin Patch

Prep time: 7 mins
Components: 1/2 cup pumpkin puree, 1 banana, 1 tsp pumpkin spice, 1 cup oat milk
Serves: 1
Cooking technique: Blending
Steps: Place pumpkin puree, a peeled and sliced banana, pumpkin spice, and oat milk into the blender. Blend until the mixture is completely homogenous.
Nutritional composition: Fat: 1.5g, Protein: 3g, Carbs: 30g, Fiber: 5g, Vitamin A, Potassium.
Calories: 200

Recipe 3: Pecan Pie Dream

Prep time: 6 mins
Components: 1/2 cup pecans, 1 tbsp maple syrup, 1 cup cashew milk, 1/2 tsp vanilla extract
Serves: 1
Cooking technique: Blending
Steps: Add pecans, maple syrup, cashew milk, and vanilla extract to the blender. Blend until the mixture reaches a creamy consistency.

Nutritional composition: Fat: 20g, Protein: 4g, Carbs: 15g, Fiber: 3g, Healthy fats, Magnesium.
Calories: 280

Recipe 4: Sweet Potato Comfort

Prep time: 8 mins
Components: 1/2 cup sweet potato, 1 cup coconut milk, 1 tsp nutmeg, 1 tbsp brown sugar
Serves: 1
Cooking technique: Blending
Steps: Add cooked sweet potato, coconut milk, nutmeg, and brown sugar to the blender. Blend until the mixture is smooth and uniform.
Nutritional composition: Fat: 3g, Protein: 2g, Carbs: 35g, Fiber: 5g, Vitamin A, Fiber.
Calories: 220

Recipe 5: Cranberry Cheer

Prep time: 5 mins
Components: 1 cup cranberries, 1 apple, 1 tbsp agave nectar, 1 cup water
Serves: 1
Cooking technique: Blending
Steps: Core and chop the apple. Combine cranberries, chopped apple, agave nectar, and water in a blender. Blend until the mixture is smooth.

Nutritional composition: Fat: 0.3g, Protein: 0.5g, Carbs: 30g, Fiber: 4g, Vitamin C, Antioxidants.
Calories: 140

Recipe 6: Toasty Hazelnut Heaven

Prep time: 7 mins
Components: 1/2 cup hazelnuts, 1 tbsp cocoa, 1 cup soy milk, 1 tsp vanilla extract
Serves: 1
Cooking technique: Blending
Steps: Add hazelnuts, cocoa, soy milk, and vanilla extract to the blender. Blend until the mixture is perfectly smooth.
Nutritional composition: Fat: 15g, Protein: 5g, Carbs: 20g, Fiber: 3g, Healthy fats, Protein.
Calories: 260

Recipe 7: Fig & Date Delight

Prep time: 6 mins
Components: 2 figs, 4 dates, 1 cup almond milk, 1/2 tsp cinnamon
Serves: 1
Cooking technique: Blending
Steps: Place figs, dates, almond milk, and cinnamon into the blender. Blend until the mixture is completely smooth.
Nutritional composition: Fat: 1g, Protein: 2g, Carbs: 60g, Fiber: 8g, High in fiber and calcium.

Calories: 230

Recipe 8: Maple Walnut Warmth

Prep time: 5 mins

Components: 1/2 cup walnuts, 1 tbsp maple syrup, 1 cup milk, 1/2 banana

Serves: 1

Cooking technique: Blending

Steps: Combine walnuts, maple syrup, milk, and a sliced banana in the blender. Blend until the mixture reaches a rich consistency.

Nutritional composition: Fat: 18g, Protein: 5g, Carbs: 30g, Fiber: 4g, High in omega-3 and potassium.

Calories: 270

Recipe 9: Pear & Ginger Soothe

Prep time: 6 mins

Components: 1 pear, 1 tsp grated ginger, 1 tbsp honey, 1 cup water

Serves: 1

Cooking technique: Blending

Steps: Peel and core the pear, add it to the blender with grated ginger, honey, and water. Blend until the mixture is smooth.

Nutritional composition: Fat: 0.2g, Protein: 1g, Carbs: 28g, Fiber: 6g, High in vitamin C and anti-inflammatory properties.

Calories: 130

Recipe 10: Spiced Carrot Cake

Prep time: 7 mins

Components: 1/2 cup carrot juice, 1 tsp mixed spice, 1 tbsp raisins, 1 cup yogurt

Serves: 1

Cooking technique: Blending

Steps: Add carrot juice, mixed spice, raisins, and yogurt to the blender. Blend until the mixture is smooth and well-combined.

Nutritional composition: Fat: 3g, Protein: 5g, Carbs: 40g, Fiber: 3g, High in vitamin A and probiotics.

Calories: 200

Winter Soothe

Recipe 1: Vanilla Snowflake

Prep time: 5 mins

Components: 1 cup almond milk, 1 tsp vanilla extract, 1 tbsp honey, 1 frozen banana

Serves: 1

Cooking technique: Blending

Steps: Place frozen banana, almond milk, vanilla extract, and honey into the blender. Blend until the mixture is smooth and creamy.

Nutritional composition: Fat: 2g, Protein: 2g, Carbs: 30g, Fiber: 3g, High in potassium, calcium.

Calories: 180

Recipe 2: Minty Cocoa Comfort

Prep time: 7 mins

Components: 1 cup oat milk, 1 tbsp cocoa powder, 1/2 tsp peppermint extract
Serves: 1
Cooking technique: Blending
Steps: Add cocoa powder, peppermint extract, and oat milk to the blender. Blend until the texture is smooth and rich.
Nutritional composition: Fat: 2.5g, Protein: 3g, Carbs: 20g, Fiber: 4g, Rich in antioxidants, fiber.
Calories: 150

Recipe 3: Citrus Winter Bliss

Prep time: 6 mins
Components: 1 orange, 1/2 grapefruit, 1 tbsp agave syrup, 1 cup water
Serves: 1
Cooking technique: Blending
Steps: Combine peeled orange and grapefruit, agave syrup, and water in the blender. Blend until the mixture is smooth.
Nutritional composition: Fat: 0.2g, Protein: 2g, Carbs: 25g, Fiber: 5g, High in vitamin C, fiber.
Calories: 120

Recipe 4: Spiced Almond Joy

Prep time: 5 mins
Components: 1 cup almond milk, 1 tsp cinnamon, 1 tbsp almond butter
Serves: 1
Cooking technique: Blending
Steps: Add almond milk, cinnamon, and almond butter to the blender. Blend until the mixture is smooth and flavored.
Nutritional composition: Fat: 9g, Protein: 4g, Carbs: 8g, Fiber: 3g, Rich in healthy fats, protein.
Calories: 210

Recipe 5: Berry Winter Warmer

Prep time: 5 mins
Components: 1/2 cup mixed berries, 1 cup soy milk, 1 tbsp chia seeds
Serves: 1
Cooking technique: Blending
Steps: Place mixed berries, soy milk, and chia seeds in the blender. Blend until the mixture is smooth.
Nutritional composition: Fat: 4g, Protein: 6g, Carbs: 20g, Fiber: 5g, High in omega-3, antioxidants.
Calories: 190

Recipe 6: Cozy Chocolate Cherry

Prep time: 7 mins
Components: 1/2 cup of pitted cherries, 1 tbsp cocoa powder, 1 cup coconut milk
Serves: 1
Cooking technique: Blending
Steps: Combine cherries, cocoa powder, and coconut milk in the blender. Blend until the mixture is smooth and well-integrated.

Nutritional composition: Fat: 8g, Protein: 3g, Carbs: 25g, Fiber: 4g, High in vitamin C, antioxidants.
Calories: 220

Recipe 7: Nutty Caramel Hug

Prep time: 6 mins
Components: 1 tbsp peanut butter, 1 tsp caramel extract, 1 cup cashew milk
Serves: 1
Cooking technique: Blending
Steps: Add peanut butter, caramel extract, and cashew milk to the blender. Blend until the mixture is rich and smooth.
Nutritional composition: Fat: 12g, Protein: 4g, Carbs: 15g, Fiber: 1g, Rich in protein, healthy fats.
Calories: 240

Recipe 8: Gingerbread Embrace

Prep time: 5 mins
Components: 1/2 tsp ginger powder, 1 tbsp molasses, 1 cup milk, 1 tsp cinnamon
Serves: 1
Cooking technique: Blending
Steps: Combine ginger powder, molasses, milk, and cinnamon in the blender. Blend until the mixture is rich and well-combined.
Nutritional composition: Fat: 2g, Protein: 8g, Carbs: 30g, Fiber: 1g, Rich in iron, calcium.
Calories: 200

Recipe 9: Pomegranate Peace

Prep time: 6 mins
Components: 1/2 cup pomegranate seeds, 1 apple, 1 cup water
Serves: 1
Cooking technique: Blending
Steps: Add pomegranate seeds, chopped apple, and water to the blender. Blend until the mixture is smooth.
Nutritional composition: Fat: 0.5g, Protein: 1g, Carbs: 28g, Fiber: 5g, High in vitamin C, antioxidants.
Calories: 130

Recipe 10: Caramelized Pear Whisper

Prep time: 7 mins
Components: 1 pear, 1 tsp caramel extract, 1 cup Greek yogurt
Serves: 1
Cooking technique: Blending
Steps: Core and slice the pear, add it to the blender with caramel extract and Greek yogurt. Blend until the mixture is smooth and creamy.
Nutritional composition: Fat: 1g, Protein: 10g, Carbs: 35g, Fiber: 3g, High in protein, vitamin C.
Calories: 220

CHAPTER 4: Weight Loss Smoothie Recipes

Recipe 1: Green Apple Metabolism Booster

Prep time: 5 minutes

Components: 1 whole green apple (cored, sliced), 1 cup spinach, 1/2 cucumber (sliced), 1 tbsp lemon juice, 1/2 inch ginger (peeled), 1 cup water

Serves: 1

Cooking technique: Blending

Steps: Wash and slice the green apple and cucumber, peel the ginger. Combine the sliced apple, spinach, sliced cucumber, lemon juice, peeled ginger, and water in a blender. Blend until the mixture is smooth.

Nutritional composition: Carbs: 31g, Protein: 2g, Fat: 0.5g, Fiber: 6g, Vitamin A: 2813 IU, Vitamin C: 36mg

Calories: 120

Recipe 2: Berry Protein Fusion

Prep time: 5 minutes

Components: 1 cup mixed berries, 1/2 cup Greek yogurt, 1/2 cup almond milk, 1 tbsp chia seeds

Serves: 1

Cooking technique: Blending

Steps: Blend mixed berries, Greek yogurt, and almond milk until smooth. Stir in chia seeds after blending for a crunchy texture.

Nutritional composition: Carbs: 24g, Protein: 10g, Fat: 4g, Fiber: 7g, Calcium: 150mg, Vitamin C: 21mg

Calories: 150

Recipe 3: Citrus Fat Burner

Prep time: 5 minutes

Components: 1 grapefruit, 1 orange, 2 tbsp lemon juice, 1 tsp honey, 1/2 cup ice cubes

Serves: 1

Cooking technique: Blending

Steps: Peel the grapefruit and orange. Combine the peeled fruits with lemon juice, honey, and ice cubes in the blender. Blend until smooth.

Nutritional composition: Carbs: 26g, Protein: 2g, Fat: 0.3g, Fiber: 4g, Potassium: 400mg, Vitamin C: 117mg

Calories: 130

Recipe 4: Spicy Avocado Slimmer

Prep time: 5 minutes

Components: 1/4 avocado, 1 cup spinach, 1/8 tsp cayenne pepper, 3/4 cup almond milk, 1 tsp lime juice

Serves: 1

Cooking technique: Blending

Steps: Add the avocado, spinach, cayenne pepper, almond milk, and lime juice into the blender. Blend until the mixture achieves a smooth texture.

Nutritional composition: Carbs: 9g, Protein: 3g, Fat: 7g, Fiber: 7g, Vitamin K: 483mcg, Vitamin C: 24mg

Calories: 110

Recipe 5: Green Tea Metabolism Mixer

Prep time: 5 minutes

Components: 1 cup brewed green tea (cooled), 1 green apple (chopped), 1 inch ginger (peeled), 1/4 cup parsley, 2 tbsp lemon juice

Serves: 1

Cooking technique: Blending

Steps: Combine brewed green tea (cooled), chopped green apple, peeled ginger, parsley, and lemon juice in the blender. Blend until smooth.

Nutritional composition: Carbs: 22g, Protein: 1g, Fat: 0.2g, Fiber: 5g, Iron: 1.2mg, Vitamin C: 18mg

Calories: 100

Recipe 6: Carrot Ginger Glow

Prep time: 5 minutes

Components: 2 medium carrots (chopped), 1/2 inch ginger (peeled), 1 medium apple (cored and sliced), 2 tbsp lemon juice, 1 cup water

Serves: 1

Cooking technique: Blending

Steps: Peel and chop the carrots and ginger, and core and slice the apple. Place the chopped carrots, peeled ginger, sliced apple, lemon juice, and water in the blender. Blend until smooth.

Nutritional composition: Carbs: 25g, Protein: 1g, Fat: 0.2g, Fiber: 6g, Vitamin A: 21383 IU, Vitamin C: 14mg

Calories: 110

Recipe 7: Tropical Turmeric Tonic

Prep time: 5 minutes

Components: 1 cup frozen or fresh pineapple (chopped), 1/2 cup frozen or fresh mango (chopped), 1/2 tsp turmeric, 1 cup coconut water

Serves: 1

Cooking technique: Blending

Steps: Chop the pineapple and mango. Combine the chopped pineapple, chopped mango, turmeric, and coconut water in the blender. Blend until smooth.

Nutritional composition: Carbs: 33g, Protein: 2g, Fat: 0.5g, Fiber: 4g, Vitamin C: 89mg, Vitamin A: 1080 IU

Calories: 140

Recipe 8: Kale and Kiwi Kickstart

Prep time: 5 minutes
Components: 1 cup kale (chopped), 1 kiwi (peeled and sliced), 1/2 banana, 1 tsp flaxseed, 3/4 cup almond milk
Serves: 1
Cooking technique: Blending
Steps: Chop the kale, peel and slice the kiwi, and slice the banana. Add the chopped kale, sliced kiwi, sliced banana, flaxseed, and almond milk into the blender. Blend until smooth.
Nutritional composition: Carbs: 27g, Protein: 3g, Fat: 3g, Fiber: 6g, Vitamin C: 95mg, Calcium: 179mg
Calories: 140

Recipe 9: Blueberry Blast

Prep time: 5 minutes
Components: 1/2 cup blueberries, 1 cup spinach, 1/4 cup Greek yogurt, 3/4 cup almond milk, 1/8 tsp cinnamon
Serves: 1
Cooking technique: Blending
Steps: Add blueberries, spinach, Greek yogurt, almond milk, and cinnamon to the blender. Blend until smooth.
Nutritional composition: Carbs: 18g, Protein: 5g, Fat: 2g, Fiber: 4g, Vitamin C: 24mg, Calcium: 185mg
Calories: 110

Recipe 10: Sweet Spinach Slimmer

Prep time: 5 minutes
Components: 1 cup spinach, 1 medium apple (cored and sliced), 2 celery stalks (chopped), 2 tbsp lemon juice, 1 cup water
Serves: 1
Cooking technique: Blending
Steps: Core and slice the apple, finely chop the celery. Combine spinach, sliced apple, chopped celery, lemon juice, and water in the blender. Blend until smooth.
Nutritional composition: Carbs: 28g, Protein: 2g, Fat: 0.5g, Fiber: 6g, Vitamin A: 5626 IU, Vitamin C: 22mg
Calories: 120

Recipe 11: Minty Melon Refresh

Prep time: 5 minutes
Components: 2 cups watermelon (cubed), 1/4 cup mint leaves, 1/2 cucumber (sliced), 2 tbsp lime juice, 1 cup ice
Serves: 1
Cooking technique: Blending
Steps: Cube the watermelon and slice the cucumber. Combine watermelon cubes, mint leaves, sliced cucumber, lime juice, and ice in the blender. Blend until refreshing.

Nutritional composition: Carbs: 25g, Protein: 2g, Fat: 0.5g, Fiber: 2g, Vitamin A: 865 IU, Vitamin C: 28mg
Calories: 100

Recipe 12: Protein Pumpkin Patch

Prep time: 5 minutes
Components: 1/4 cup pumpkin puree, 1/2 scoop vanilla protein powder, 3/4 cup almond milk, 1/8 tsp nutmeg, 1/8 tsp cinnamon
Serves: 1
Cooking technique: Blending
Steps: Combine pumpkin puree, vanilla protein powder, almond milk, nutmeg, and cinnamon in the blender. Blend until creamy and smooth.
Nutritional composition: Carbs: 15g, Protein: 12g, Fat: 2g, Fiber: 3g, Vitamin A: 7633 IU, Vitamin C: 2mg
Calories: 120

Recipe 13: Zesty Lemon Cleanse

Prep time: 5 minutes
Components: 1 lemon (juiced), 1 medium apple (cored and sliced), 1/2 inch ginger (peeled), 1 cup spinach, 1 cup water
Serves: 1
Cooking technique: Blending
Step Juice the lemon, core and slice the apple, peel the ginger. Combine lemon juice, sliced apple, peeled ginger, spinach, and water in the blender. Blend until completely smooth.
Nutritional composition: Carbs: 25g, Protein: 2g, Fat: 0.3g, Fiber: 5g, Vitamin C: 44mg, Iron: 1.5mg
Calories: 100

Recipe 14: Choco Almond Dream

Prep time: 5 minutes
Components: 1 tbsp unsweetened cocoa powder, 1 tsp almond butter, 1/2 banana, 3/4 cup almond milk, 1/2 tbsp chia seeds
Serves: 1
Cooking technique: Blending
Steps: Add unsweetened cocoa powder, almond butter, banana, and chia seeds to your blender. Pour in almond milk. Blend everything until the texture becomes smooth and creamy.
Nutritional composition: Carbs: 25g, Protein: 5g, Fat: 8g, Fiber: 7g, Calcium: 189mg, Iron: 2mg
Calories: 170

Recipe 15: Beetroot Bliss

Prep time: 5 minutes
Components: 1 cooked beetroot (peeled and chopped), 1 carrot (chopped), 1 apple (cored and sliced), 1/2 inch ginger (peeled), 1 cup water

Serves: 1

Cooking technique: Blending

Steps: Peel and chop the cooked beetroot, carrot, and ginger, core and slice the apple. Combine chopped beetroot, chopped carrot, sliced apple, peeled ginger, and water in the blender. Blend until smooth.

Nutritional composition: Carbs: 35g, Protein: 2g, Fat: 0.4g, Fiber: 8g, Vitamin A: 11089 IU, Vitamin C: 14mg

Calories: 140

Recipe 16: Strawberry Basil Booster

Prep time: 5 minutes

Components: 1/2 cup strawberries, 2 tbsp basil leaves, 1/4 cup Greek yogurt, 1 tsp honey, 1 tbsp lemon juice

Serves: 1

Cooking technique: Blending

Steps: Combine strawberries, basil leaves, Greek yogurt, honey, and lemon juice in the blender. Blend until smooth.

Nutritional composition: Carbs: 14g, Protein: 5g, Fat: 0.3g, Fiber: 2g, Vitamin C: 49mg, Calcium: 96mg

Calories: 80

Recipe 17: Apple Cinnamon Delight

Prep time: 5 minutes

Components: 1/2 medium apple, 1/4 tsp cinnamon, 1/4 cup Greek yogurt, 3/4 cup almond milk, 1/2 tbsp honey

Serves: 1

Cooking technique: Blending

Steps: Core and slice the apple. Add the sliced apple, cinnamon, Greek yogurt, almond milk, and honey to the blender. Blend until smooth.

Nutritional composition: Carbs: 18g, Protein: 4g, Fat: 1.25g, Fiber: 3g, Calcium: 150mg, Vitamin C: 4mg

Calories: 100

Recipe 18: Pineapple Paradise

Prep time: 5 minutes

Components: 1 cup pineapple (chopped), 1 cup spinach, 1/2 cucumber (sliced), 1 cup coconut water

Serves: 1

Cooking technique: Blending

Steps: Chop the pineapple, slice the cucumber. Combine chopped pineapple, spinach, sliced cucumber, and coconut water in the blender. Blend until smooth.

Nutritional composition: Carbs: 25g, Protein: 3g, Fat: 0.5g, Fiber: 5g, Vitamin C: 79mg, Manganese: 1.2mg

Calories: 120

Recipe 19: Raspberry Refresher

Prep time: 5 minutes

Components: 1/2 cup raspberries, 2 tbsp mint leaves, 1/4 cup Greek yogurt, 1 tbsp lemon juice, 1/2 tbsp honey

Serves: 1

Cooking technique: Blending

Steps: Combine raspberries, mint leaves, Greek yogurt, lemon juice, and honey in the blender. Blend until smooth.

Nutritional composition: Carbs: 16g, Protein: 4g, Fat: 0.5g, Fiber: 4g, Vitamin C: 25mg, Magnesium: 27mg

Calories: 90

Recipe 20: Savory Spinach and Avocado

Prep time: 5 minutes

Components: 1 cup spinach, 1/4 avocado, 1/2 cucumber, 1/4 cup Greek yogurt, 1 tbsp lemon juice

Serves: 1

Cooking technique: Blending

Steps: Chop the cucumber. Combine spinach, avocado, chopped cucumber, Greek yogurt, and lemon juice in the blender. Blend until creamy.

Nutritional composition: Carbs: 7.5g, Protein: 2.5g, Fat: 7.5g, Fiber: 5g, Vitamin K: 482mcg, Vitamin C: 17mg

Calories: 110

CHAPTER 5: Energy-Boosting Smoothie Recipes

Recipe 1: Protein Powerhouse

Prep time: 5 mins

Components: 1 banana, 1 scoop protein powder, 1 cup almond milk

Serves: 1

Cooking technique: Blending

Steps: Peel the banana. Combine the peeled banana, protein powder, and almond milk in a blender. Blend until the mixture is smooth.

Nutritional composition: Fat: 2g, Protein: 20g, Carbs: 30g, High in potassium.

Calories: 260

Recipe 2: Greek Yogurt Citrus Zing

Prep time: 6 mins

Components: 1 orange, 1 cup Greek yogurt, 1 tbsp honey

Serves: 1

Cooking technique: Blending

Steps: Peel the orange. Add the peeled orange, Greek yogurt, and honey to the blender. Blend until the mixture is smooth.

Nutritional composition: Fat: 1g, Protein: 20g, Carbs: 25g, High in Vitamin C.

Calories: 220

Recipe 3: Berry Quinoa Boost

Prep time: 7 mins

Components: 1/2 cup mixed berries, 1 cup coconut water, 1/4 cup cooked quinoa

Serves: 1

Cooking technique: Blending

Steps: Ensure the quinoa is cooked and cooled. Add the mixed berries, coconut water, and cooked quinoa to the blender. Blend until smooth.

Nutritional composition: Fat: 1g, Protein: 5g, Carbs: 30g, High in antioxidants.

Calories: 180

Recipe 4: Spinach Tofu Energizer

Prep time: 6 mins

Components: 1 cup spinach, 1/2 cup silken tofu, 1 cup water

Serves: 1

Cooking technique: Blending

Steps: Add spinach, silken tofu, and water to the blender. Blend until the mixture is completely smooth.

Nutritional composition: Fat: 2g, Protein: 10g, Carbs: 5g, High in Vitamins A & C.

Calories: 120

Recipe 5: Tropical Lentil Bliss

Prep time: 8 mins

Components: 1/2 cup mango, 1/4 cup cooked red lentils, 1 cup coconut milk

Serves: 1

Cooking technique: Blending

Steps: Ensure the lentils are cooked and cooled. Add mango, cooked red lentils, and coconut milk to the blender. Blend until smooth.

Nutritional composition: Fat: 5g, Protein: 10g, Carbs: 30g, High in Vitamin A.

Calories: 250

Recipe 6: Almond Chickpea Fusion

Prep time: 7 mins

Components: 1/4 cup chickpeas, 1 tbsp almond butter, 1 cup almond milk

Serves: 1

Cooking technique: Blending

Steps: Ensure the chickpeas are cooked and rinsed. Add chickpeas, almond butter, and almond milk to the blender. Blend until the mixture is creamy.

Nutritional composition: Fat: 14g, Protein: 10g, Carbs: 20g, Rich in healthy fats.

Calories: 280

Recipe 7: Spicy Ginger Protein Kick

Prep time: 6 mins

Components: 1 tsp ginger, 1 apple, 1 scoop protein powder, 1 cup water

Serves: 1

Cooking technique: Blending

Steps: Peel the apple and ginger. Add the peeled ginger, apple, protein powder, and water to the blender. Blend until smooth.

Nutritional composition: Fat: 1g, Protein: 20g, Carbs: 25g, High in Vitamin C.

Calories: 220

Recipe 8: Peanut Butter Banana Delight

Prep time: 5 mins

Components: 1 banana, 2 tbsp peanut butter, 1 cup soy milk

Serves: 1

Cooking technique: Blending

Steps: Peel the banana. Add the banana, peanut butter, and soy milk to the blender. Blend until smooth.

Nutritional composition: Fat: 16g, Protein: 15g, Carbs: 35g, Rich in potassium.

Calories: 350

Recipe 9: Oatmeal Cinnamon Protein Rush

Prep time: 6 mins
Components: 1/2 cup oats, 1 scoop protein powder, 1 tsp cinnamon, 1 cup milk
Serves: 1
Cooking technique: Blending
Steps: Add oats, protein powder, cinnamon, and milk to the blender. Blend until the mixture reaches a consistent texture.
Nutritional composition: Fat: 3g, Protein: 25g, Carbs: 40g, High in fiber and calcium.
Calories: 300

Recipe 10: Peachy Protein Power

Prep time: 5 mins
Components: 1 peach, 1 cup Greek yogurt, 1 scoop protein powder
Serves: 1
Cooking technique: Blending
Steps: Peel and chop the peach. Add the chopped peach, Greek yogurt, and protein powder to the blender. Blend until smooth.
Nutritional composition: Fat: 1g, Protein: 25g, Carbs: 30g, High in Vitamin C.
Calories: 270

Recipe 11: Kiwi Kale Edamame Charge

Prep time: 6 mins
Components: 1 kiwi, 1 cup kale, 1/4 cup shelled edamame, 1 cup water
Serves: 1
Cooking technique: Blending
Steps: Peel the kiwi. Combine kiwi, kale, edamame (ensure they are shelled), and water in the blender. Blend until smooth.
Nutritional composition: Fat: 2g, Protein: 10g, Carbs: 20g, High in Vitamin K and C.
Calories: 150

Recipe 12: Cocoa Almond Lift

Prep time: 5 mins
Components: 1 tbsp cocoa powder, 2 tbsp almond butter, 1 scoop protein powder, 1 cup almond milk
Serves: 1
Cooking technique: Blending
Steps: Add cocoa powder, almond butter, protein powder, and almond milk to the blender. Blend well to combine all ingredients into a smooth mixture.
Nutritional composition: Fat: 15g, Protein: 20g, Carbs: 20g, High in magnesium.
Calories: 320

Recipe 13: Pomegranate Pumpkin Seed Punch

Prep time: 7 mins

Components: 1/2 cup pomegranate seeds, 1 tbsp pumpkin seeds, 1 scoop protein powder, 1 cup water

Serves: 1

Cooking technique: Blending

Steps: Add pomegranate seeds, pumpkin seeds, protein powder, and water to the blender. Blend until smooth.

Nutritional composition: Fat: 4g, Protein: 15g, Carbs: 20g, Rich in antioxidants.

Calories: 200

Recipe 14: Pineapple Spirulina Surge

Prep time: 5 mins

Components: 1/2 cup pineapple, 1 tsp spirulina, 1 scoop protein powder, 1 cup coconut water

Serves: 1

Cooking technique: Blending

Steps: Chop the pineapple. Add the chopped pineapple, spirulina, protein powder, and coconut water to the blender. Blend until smooth.

Nutritional composition: Fat: 1g, Protein: 20g, Carbs: 25g, High in Vitamin C.

Calories: 220

Recipe 15: Chia Cherry Charge

Prep time: 5 mins

Components: 1/2 cup of pitted cherries, 2 tbsp chia seeds, 1 scoop protein powder, 1 cup almond milk

Serves: 1

Cooking technique: Blending

Steps: Add cherries, chia seeds, protein powder, and almond milk to the blender. Blend until smooth, then allow the mixture to sit for 2 minutes to thicken slightly due to the chia seeds.

Nutritional composition: Fat: 9g, Protein: 20g, Carbs: 25g, High in Omega-3.

Calories: 240

Recipe 16: Mocha Hemp Elevation

Prep time: 7 mins

Components: 1 cup brewed coffee (cooled), 1 tbsp cocoa powder, 2 tbsp hemp seeds, 1 cup milk

Serves: 1

Cooking technique: Blending

Steps: Combine brewed coffee (cooled), cocoa powder, hemp seeds, and milk in the blender. Blend until smooth.

Nutritional composition: Fat: 8g, Protein: 15g, Carbs: 20g, Rich in antioxidants.

Calories: 250

Recipe 17: Pineapple Tempeh Triumph

Prep time: 5 mins

Components: 1/2 cup pineapple, 1/4 cup tempeh, 1 cup coconut water

Serves: 1

Cooking technique: Blending

Steps: Chop the pineapple and tempeh. Add chopped pineapple, chopped tempeh, and coconut water to the blender. Blend until smooth.

Nutritional composition: Fat: 5g, Protein: 15g, Carbs: 20g, High in Vitamin C.

Calories: 180

CHAPTER 6: Vegetarian and Vegan Smoothie Recipes

Recipe 1: Green Machine

Recipe 1: Green Machine

Prep time: 5 mins

Components: 1 cup spinach, 1 green apple, 1 cup almond milk

Serves: 1

Cooking technique: Blending

Steps: Wash and core the green apple, then chop it. Add the chopped apple, spinach, and almond milk to the blender. Blend until the mixture is completely smooth.

Nutritional composition: Fat: 0.5g, Protein: 1g, Carbs: 25g, High in Vitamins A and C.

Calories: 150

Recipe 2: Soy Berry Bliss

Prep time: 6 mins

Components: 1/2 cup mixed berries, 1 cup soy milk

Serves: 1

Cooking technique: Blending

Steps: Add the mixed berries and soy milk to the blender. Blend until you achieve a smooth, creamy consistency.

Nutritional composition: Fat: 2g, Protein: 6g, Carbs: 20g, High in antioxidants and Vitamin C.

Calories: 120

Recipe 3: Mango Tango

Prep time: 5 mins

Components: 1 ripe mango, 1 cup coconut water

Serves: 1

Cooking technique: Blending

Steps: Peel and chop the mango. Add the chopped mango and coconut water to the blender. Blend until completely smooth.

Nutritional composition: Fat: 0.3g, Protein: 1g, Carbs: 30g, High in Vitamin C and Hydration.

Calories: 130

Recipe 4: Spicy Carrot Cooler

Prep time: 7 mins

Components: 2 carrots, pinch of cayenne pepper, 1 cup water

Serves: 1

Cooking technique: Blending

Steps: Peel and chop the carrots. Add the chopped carrots, a pinch of cayenne pepper, and water to the blender. Blend until smooth.

Nutritional composition: Fat: 0.2g, Protein: 1g, Carbs: 25g, High in Beta-carotene and Spice.

Calories: 60

Recipe 5: Walnut Wonder with banana

Prep time: 6 mins

Components: 2 tbsp walnuts, 1 banana, 1 cup almond milk

Serves: 1

Cooking technique: Blending

Steps: Chop the banana. Add the chopped banana, walnuts, and almond milk to the blender. Blend until smooth.

Nutritional composition: Fat: 10g, Protein: 3g, Carbs: 30g, High in Omega-3 and Potassium.

Calories: 250

Recipe 6: Pumpkin Pleasure

Prep time: 7 mins

Components: 1/2 cup pumpkin puree, 1 tsp cinnamon, 1 cup soy milk

Serves: 1

Cooking technique: Blending

Steps: Combine pumpkin puree, cinnamon, and soy milk in the blender. Blend until the mixture is smooth.

Nutritional composition: Fat: 1.5g, Protein: 5g, Carbs: 20g, High in Beta-carotene and Spices.

Calories: 180

Recipe 7: Sweet Beet Retreat

Prep time: 8 mins

Components: 1 beetroot, 1 tsp agave nectar, 1 cup coconut water

Serves: 1

Cooking technique: Blending

Steps: Peel, chop the beetroot, then blend it with agave nectar and coconut water to a consistent texture.

Nutritional composition: Fat: 0.1g, Protein: 2g, Carbs: 25g, High in Folate and Natural sugars.

Calories: 140

Recipe 8: Cacao Cashew Bliss

Prep time: 6 mins

Components: 1 tbsp cacao nibs, 2 tbsp cashew butter, 1 cup almond milk

Serves: 1

Cooking technique: Blending

Steps: Add cacao nibs, cashew butter, and almond milk to the blender. Blend until the mixture is smooth and well-integrated.

Nutritional composition: Fat: 15g, Protein: 5g, Carbs: 20g, High in Magnesium and Healthy fats.

Calories: 280

Recipe 9: Raspberry Chia Harmony

Prep time: 5 mins

Components: 1/2 cup raspberries, 2 tbsp chia seeds, 1 cup water

Serves: 1

Cooking technique: Blending

Steps: Add raspberries, chia seeds, and water to the blender. Blend until smooth, then let the mixture sit for 2 minutes to allow the chia seeds to expand slightly.

Nutritional composition: Fat: 5g, Protein: 3g, Carbs: 20g, High in Omega-3 and Fiber.

Calories: 120

Recipe 10: Zesty Lime Lullaby

Prep time: 5 mins

Components: Juice of 2 limes, 1 tsp agave nectar, 1 cup coconut water

Serves: 1

Cooking technique: Blending

Steps: Juice the limes. Add lime juice, agave nectar, and coconut water to the blender. Blend until the mixture is smooth.

Nutritional composition: Fat: 0g, Protein: 0.5g, Carbs: 20g, High in Vitamin C and Hydration.

Calories: 90

Recipe 11: Turmeric Ginger Soothe

Prep time: 7 mins

Components: 1 tsp turmeric, 1/2 tsp ginger, 1 cup soy milk

Serves: 1

Cooking technique: Blending

Steps: Add turmeric, ginger, and soy milk to the blender. Blend until the mixture is smooth and evenly mixed.

Nutritional composition: Fat: 2g, Protein: 6g, Carbs: 10g, High in Anti-inflammatory properties and Spices.

Calories: 100

Recipe 12: Avocado Aloe Elixir

Prep time: 6 mins

Components: 1/2 avocado, 2 tbsp aloe vera juice, 1 cup almond milk

Serves: 1

Cooking technique: Blending

Steps: Peel and pit the avocado. Add the avocado, aloe vera juice, and almond milk to the blender. Blend until smooth.

Nutritional composition: Fat: 15g, Protein: 2g, Carbs: 10g, High in Healthy fats and Vitamins.

Calories: 220

Recipe 13: Papaya Passion

Prep time: 5 mins

Components: 1/2 papaya, 1 cup coconut water

Serves: 1

Cooking technique: Blending

Steps: Peel and seed the papaya, then chop it. Add the chopped papaya and coconut water to the blender. Blend until smooth.

Nutritional composition: Fat: 0.3g, Protein: 1g, Carbs: 25g, High in Vitamin C and Hydration.

Calories: 110

Recipe 14: Matcha Mint Marvel

Prep time: 6 mins

Components: 1 tsp matcha powder, handful of mint leaves, 1 cup soy milk

Serves: 1

Cooking technique: Blending

Steps: Wash the mint leaves thoroughly. Add matcha powder, cleaned mint leaves, and soy milk to the blender. Blend until the mixture is smooth and the mint is evenly distributed.

Nutritional composition: Fat: 2g, Protein: 6g, Carbs: 15g, High in Antioxidants and Refreshing properties.

Calories: 90

Recipe 15: Blueberry Basil Burst

Prep time: 5 mins

Components: 1/2 cup blueberries, handful of basil leaves, 1 cup water

Serves: 1

Cooking technique: Blending

Steps: Add blueberries, basil leaves, and water to the blender. Blend until smooth.

Nutritional composition: Fat: 0.5g, Protein: 1g, Carbs: 15g, High in Antioxidants and Refreshing taste.

Calories: 70

Recipe 16: Pineapple Coconut Oasis

Prep time: 7 mins

Components: 1/2 cup pineapple, 2 tbsp coconut flakes, 1 cup coconut water

Serves: 1

Cooking technique: Blending

Steps: Chop the pineapple. Add the chopped pineapple, coconut flakes, and coconut water to the blender. Blend until smooth.

Nutritional composition: Fat: 5g, Protein: 1g, Carbs: 25g, High in Vitamin C and Healthy fats.

Calories: 150

Recipe 17: Golden Grapefruit Glow

Prep time: 5 mins

Components: 1 grapefruit, 1 tsp agave nectar, 1 cup water

Serves: 1

Cooking technique: Blending

Steps: Peel and seed the grapefruit, then chop it. Add the chopped grapefruit, agave nectar, and water to the blender. Blend until smooth.

Nutritional composition: Fat: 0.2g, Protein: 1g, Carbs: 20g, High in Vitamin C and Natural sugars.
Calories: 110

CHAPTER 7: Cleansing Smoothie Recipes

Recipe 1: Citrus Cleanse

Prep time: 5 mins

Components: 1 grapefruit, 1 orange, 1 cup water

Serves: 1

Cooking technique: Blending

Steps: Peel the grapefruit and orange. Combine the grapefruit, orange, and water in a blender; blend until smooth.

Nutritional composition: Fat: 0g, Protein: 2g, Carbs: 30g, High in Vitamin C and Antioxidants.

Calories: 130

Recipe 2: Celery Symphony

Prep time: 5 mins

Components: 3 celery stalks, 1 green apple, 1 cup coconut water

Serves: 1

Cooking technique: Blending

Steps: Wash and chop the celery stalks and green apple. Add the celery, apple, and coconut water to the blender; blend until smooth.

Nutritional composition: Fat: 0.5g, Protein: 1g, Carbs: 20g, High in Vitamins and Hydration.

Calories: 90

Recipe 3: Ginger Glow

Prep time: 6 mins

Components: 1 inch ginger, 1 pear, 1 cup water

Serves: 1

Cooking technique: Blending

Steps: Peel and chop the ginger and pear. Combine the ginger, pear, and water in the blender; blend until smooth.

Nutritional composition: Fat: 0.3g, Protein: 1g, Carbs: 25g, High in Anti-inflammatory properties and Vitamins.

Calories: 100

Recipe 4: Cucumber Calm

Prep time: 5 mins

Components: 1 cucumber, 1 tbsp honey, 1 cup water

Serves: 1

Cooking technique: Blending

Steps: Wash and chop the cucumber. Combine the cucumber, honey, and water in the blender; blend until smooth.

Nutritional composition: Fat: 0.2g, Protein: 2g, Carbs: 15g, High in Hydration and Minerals.

Calories: 80

Recipe 5: Dandelion Detox

Prep time: 7 mins
Components: 1 cup dandelion greens, 1 lemon, 1 cup water
Serves: 1
Cooking technique: Blending
Steps: Wash the dandelion greens thoroughly. Juice the lemon. Combine the dandelion greens, lemon juice, and water in the blender; blend until smooth.
Nutritional composition: Fat: 0.5g, Protein: 2g, Carbs: 10g, High in Vitamins A and C.
Calories: 50

Recipe 6: Coconut Watermelon Wave

Prep time: 5 mins
Components: 2 cups watermelon, 1 tbsp chia seeds, 1 cup coconut water
Serves: 1
Cooking technique: Blending
Steps: Chop the watermelon. Add the watermelon, chia seeds, and coconut water to the blender; blend until smooth.
Nutritional composition: Fat: 2g, Protein: 2g, Carbs: 25g, High in Hydration and Omega-3.
Calories: 120

Recipe 7: Kale Kickstart

Prep time: 6 mins
Components: 1 cup kale, 1/2 lemon, 1 cup water
Serves: 1
Cooking technique: Blending
Steps: Wash and chop the kale. Juice the lemon. Add the kale, lemon juice, and water to the blender; blend until smooth.
Nutritional composition: Fat: 0.5g, Protein: 3g, Carbs: 10g, High in Vitamins and Minerals.
Calories: 60

Recipe 8: Charcoal Clarity

Prep time: 5 mins
Components: 1 tsp activated charcoal, 1 banana, 1 cup almond milk
Serves: 1
Cooking technique: Blending
Steps: Peel and chop the banana. Add the activated charcoal, banana, and almond milk to the blender; blend until smooth.
Nutritional composition: Fat: 3g, Protein: 2g, Carbs: 30g, High in Detoxifying properties and Potassium.
Calories: 200

Recipe 9: Pineapple Purity

Prep time: 6 mins
Components: 1 cup pineapple, 1 tbsp flax seeds, 1 cup water
Serves: 1

Cooking technique: Blending

Steps: Chop the pineapple. Combine the pineapple, flax seeds, and water in the blender; blend until smooth.

Nutritional composition: Fat: 2g, Protein: 2g, Carbs: 25g, High in Vitamin C and Omega-3.

Calories: 120

Recipe 10: Fennel Freshness

Prep time: 7 mins

Components: 1 fennel bulb, 1 green apple, 1 cup water

Serves: 1

Cooking technique: Blending

Steps: Wash and chop the fennel bulb and green apple. Add the fennel, apple, and water to the blender; blend until smooth.

Nutritional composition: Fat: 0.5g, Protein: 2g, Carbs: 20g, High in Vitamins and Digestive aid.

Calories: 100

Recipe 11: Spirulina Surge

Prep time: 5 mins

Components: 1 tsp spirulina, 1 cup spinach, 1 cup coconut water

Serves: 1

Cooking technique: Blending

Steps: Add the spirulina, spinach, and coconut water to the blender; blend until smooth.

Nutritional composition: Fat: 1g, Protein: 4g, Carbs: 15g, High in Protein and Vitamins.

Calories: 90

Recipe 12: Acai Awakening

Prep time: 6 mins

Components: 1 tbsp acai powder, 1 banana, 1 cup almond milk

Serves: 1

Cooking technique: Blending

Steps: Peel and chop the banana. Combine the acai powder, banana, and almond milk in the blender; blend until smooth.

Nutritional composition: Fat: 3g, Protein: 2g, Carbs: 30g, High in Antioxidants and Vitamins.

Calories: 200

Recipe 13: Turmeric Tonic

Prep time: 5 mins

Components: 1 tsp turmeric, 1/2 lemon, 1 cup water

Serves: 1

Cooking technique: Blending

Steps: Juice the lemon. Combine the turmeric, lemon juice, and water in the blender; blend until smooth.

Nutritional composition: Fat: 0.2g, Protein: 0.5g, Carbs: 5g, High in Anti-inflammatory properties.

Calories: 30

Recipe 14: Beetroot Bliss

Prep time: 7 mins

Components: 1 small beetroot, 1 carrot, 1 cup water

Serves: 1

Cooking technique: Blending

Steps: Peel and chop the beetroot and carrot. Add the beetroot, carrot, and water to the blender; blend until smooth.

Nutritional composition: Fat: 0.5g, Protein: 2g, Carbs: 20g, High in Vitamins A and C.

Calories: 90

Recipe 15: Parsley Purity

Prep time: 5 mins

Components: 1 cup parsley, 1 cucumber, 1 cup water

Serves: 1

Cooking technique: Blending

Steps: Wash the parsley and cucumber. Chop the cucumber. Combine the parsley, cucumber, and water in the blender; blend until smooth.

Nutritional composition: Fat: 0.5g, Protein: 2g, Carbs: 10g, High in Vitamins and Hydration.

Calories: 50

Recipe 16: Goji Grapefruit Goodness

Prep time: 6 mins

Components: 1 tbsp goji berries, 1 grapefruit, 1 cup water

Serves: 1

Cooking technique: Blending

Steps: Soak goji berries in water for a few minutes. Peel and chop the grapefruit. Combine the soaked goji berries, grapefruit, and water in the blender; blend until smooth.

Nutritional composition: Fat: 0.5g, Protein: 2g, Carbs: 25g, High in Antioxidants and Vitamin C.

Calories: 120

Recipe 17: Matcha Magic

Prep time: 5 mins

Components: 1 tsp matcha powder, 1 banana, 1 cup almond milk

Serves: 1

Cooking technique: Blending

Steps: Combine the matcha powder, peeled and chopped banana, and almond milk in the blender; blend until smooth.

Nutritional composition: Fat: 3g, Protein: 2g, Carbs: 30g, High in Antioxidants and Energy.

Calories: 180

CHAPTER 8: Gluten-Free Smoothie Recipes

Recipe 1: Simple Berry Bliss

Prep time: 5 mins
Components: 1 cup mixed berries, 1 cup almond milk
Serves: 1
Cooking technique: Blending
Steps: Blend mixed berries and almond milk until completely smooth.
Nutritional composition: Fat: 1g, Protein: 2g, Carbs: 15g, High in Antioxidants and Vitamin C.
Calories: 100

Recipe 2: Choco-Almond Delight

Prep time: 6 mins
Components: 1 tbsp cacao powder, 1 cup almond milk, 1 banana
Serves: 1
Cooking technique: Blending
Steps: Peel the banana. Add cacao powder, almond milk, and the banana to a blender and blend until well combined and smooth.
Nutritional composition: Fat: 3g, Protein: 2g, Carbs: 30g, High in Potassium and Magnesium.
Calories: 220

Recipe 3: Citrus Symphony

Prep time: 5 mins
Components: 1 orange, 1/2 grapefruit, 1 cup coconut water
Serves: 1
Cooking technique: Blending
Steps: Peel the orange and grapefruit. Combine orange, grapefruit, and coconut water in a blender and blend until smooth.
Nutritional composition: Fat: 0.5g, Protein: 2g, Carbs: 25g, High in Vitamin C and Potassium.
Calories: 120

Recipe 4: Avocado Serenity

Prep time: 5 mins
Components: 1 avocado, 1 cup water, 1 tbsp honey
Serves: 1
Cooking technique: Blending
Steps: Peel and pit the avocado. Add avocado, water, and honey to the blender and blend until smooth.
Nutritional composition: Fat: 15g, Protein: 2g, Carbs: 20g, High in Healthy Fats and Fiber.
Calories: 250

Recipe 5: Pistachio Pleasure

Prep time: 6 mins

Components: 1 tbsp pistachio butter, 1 banana, 1 cup rice milk
Serves: 1
Cooking technique: Blending
Steps: Peel the banana. Blend pistachio butter, banana, and rice milk until smooth.
Nutritional composition: Fat: 8g, Protein: 4g, Carbs: 30g, High in Protein and Vitamins.
Calories: 300

Recipe 6: Strawberry Sunrise

Prep time: 5 mins
Components: 1 cup strawberries, 1 cup oat milk
Serves: 1
Cooking technique: Blending
Steps: Blend strawberries and oat milk until they reach a smooth consistency.
Nutritional composition: Fat: 2g, Protein: 2g, Carbs: 20g, High in Vitamin C and Calcium.
Calories: 120

Recipe 7: Hazelnut Harmony

Prep time: 6 mins
Components: 1 tbsp hazelnut spread, 1 cup soy milk
Serves: 1
Cooking technique: Blending
Steps: Add hazelnut spread and soy milk to a blender and blend until smooth.
Nutritional composition: Fat: 9g, Protein: 7g, Carbs: 15g, High in Protein and Healthy fats.
Calories: 250

Recipe 8: Kiwi Kiss

Prep time: 5 mins
Components: 2 kiwis, 1 cup water
Serves: 1
Cooking technique: Blending
Steps: Peel and slice the kiwis. Add kiwis and water to a blender and blend until smooth.
Nutritional composition: Fat: 0.5g, Protein: 1g, Carbs: 15g, High in Vitamin C and Fiber.
Calories: 100

Recipe 9: Peach Perfection

Prep time: 6 mins
Components: 1 peach, 1 cup almond milk
Serves: 1
Cooking technique: Blending
Steps: Blend the peach and almond milk until smooth.
Nutritional composition: Fat: 1g, Protein: 2g, Carbs: 20g, High in Vitamin A and C.

Calories: 120 Recipe 10: Tropical Triumph

Recipe 10: Tropical Triumph

Prep time: 6 mins

Components: 1 cup pineapple, 1 cup coconut milk

Serves: 1

Cooking technique: Blending

Steps: Peel and core the pineapple, then cut it into chunks. Add the pineapple chunks and coconut milk to a blender. Blend until the mixture is completely smooth.

Nutritional composition: Fat: 5g, Protein: 2g, Carbs: 25g, High in Vitamin C and Manganese.

Calories: 230

Recipe 11: Vanilla Velvet

Prep time: 6 mins

Components: 1 tsp vanilla extract, 1 cup oat milk, 1 tbsp honey

Serves: 1

Cooking technique: Blending

Steps: Pour oat milk into the blender, add the vanilla extract, and honey. Blend until the mixture is smooth and the vanilla is completely integrated.

Nutritional composition: Fat: 5g, Protein: 2g, Carbs: 25g, High in Vitamin C and Manganese.

Calories: 230

Recipe 12: Raspberry Rapture

Prep time: 6 mins

Components: 1 cup raspberries, 1 cup soy milk

Serves: 1

Cooking technique: Blending

Steps: Wash the raspberries thoroughly under cold water. Add the clean raspberries and soy milk to a blender and blend until the mixture is smooth.

Nutritional composition: Fat: 2g, Protein: 4g, Carbs: 15g, High in Vitamin C and Fiber.

Calories: 130

Recipe 13: Lychee Luxury

Prep time: 5 mins

Components: 1 cup lychee, 1 cup rice milk

Serves: 1

Cooking technique: Blending

Steps: Peel and pit the lychees. Add the prepared lychee and rice milk to a blender and blend until smooth.

Nutritional composition: Fat: 0.5g, Protein: 1g, Carbs: 30g, High in Vitamin C and Copper.

Calories: 160

Recipe 14: Cashew Charm

Prep time: 6 mins
Components: 1 tbsp cashew butter, 1 cup almond milk
Serves: 1
Cooking technique: Blending
Steps: Add cashew butter and almond milk to a blender and process until the mixture is completely smooth.
Nutritional composition: Fat: 10g, Protein: 5g, Carbs: 10g, High in Healthy Fats and Protein.
Calories: 250

Recipe 15: Blueberry Burst

Prep time: 5 mins
Components: 1 cup blueberries, 1 cup water
Serves: 1
Cooking technique: Blending
Steps: Rinse the blueberries under cold water to remove any dirt or debris. Combine the clean blueberries and water in a blender and blend until smooth.
Nutritional composition: Fat: 0.5g, Protein: 1g, Carbs: 15g, High in Antioxidants and Vitamin C.
Calories: 100

Recipe 16: Pomegranate Purity

Prep time: 6 mins
Components: 1 cup pomegranate seeds, 1 cup coconut milk
Serves: 1
Cooking technique: Blending
Steps: Extract the seeds from the pomegranate. Add the pomegranate seeds and coconut milk to a blender and blend until smooth.
Nutritional composition: Fat: 5g, Protein: 2g, Carbs: 25g, High in Antioxidants and Vitamin C.
Calories: 200

Recipe 17: Cinnamon Cradle

Prep time: 5 mins
Components: 1 tsp cinnamon, 1 banana, 1 cup almond milk
Serves: 1
Cooking technique: Blending
Steps: Add cinnamon, a peeled and sliced banana, and almond milk to a blender. Blend until the mixture achieves a smooth consistency.
Nutritional composition: Fat: 1g, Protein: 2g, Carbs: 25g, High in Antioxidants and Fiber.
Calories: 210

CHAPTER 9: Lactose-Free Smoothie Recipes

Recipe 1: Honey Berry Bliss

Prep time: 5 mins

Components: 1 cup mixed berries, 1 cup almond milk, 1 tbsp honey

Serves: 1

Cooking technique: Blending

Steps: Add mixed berries, almond milk, and honey to a blender; blend until the mixture achieves a uniform, creamy texture.

Nutritional composition: Fat: 1.5g, Protein: 2g, Carbs: 25g, Rich in Vitamin C and Antioxidants, Calcium: 20% DV.

Calories: 130

Recipe 2: Tropical Zest

Prep time: 5 mins

Components: 1 cup pineapple, 1 cup coconut milk, 1 tsp chia seeds

Serves: 1

Cooking technique: Blending

Steps: Combine pineapple and coconut milk in a blender; blend until smooth. Stir in chia seeds after blending for a slightly textured drink, ensuring they are evenly distributed.

Nutritional composition: Fat: 5g, Protein: 2g, Carbs: 30g, Rich in Fiber, Vitamin C: 60% DV.

Calories: 180

Recipe 3: Minty Cucumber Refresher

Prep time: 7 mins

Components: 1 cucumber, 10 mint leaves, 1 cup water, 1 tbsp agave syrup

Serves: 2

Cooking technique: Blending

Steps: Wash and slice the cucumber. Blend cucumber, fresh mint leaves, water, and agave syrup until smooth.

Nutritional composition: Fat: 0.2g, Protein: 1g, Carbs: 10g, High in Vitamin K, Excellent for Hydration.

Calories: 50 per serving

Recipe 4: Spicy Ginger Pineapple

Prep time: 5 mins

Components: 1 cup pineapple, 1 tsp fresh ginger, 1 cup rice milk

Serves: 1

Cooking technique: Blending

Steps: Peel and grate fresh ginger. Add pineapple, grated ginger, and rice milk to the blender; blend until creamy.

Nutritional composition: Fat: 1g, Protein: 2g, Carbs: 22g, Rich in Vitamin C, Excellent Anti-inflammatory Properties.

Calories: 120

Recipe 5: Pomegranate Passion with juice

Prep time: 6 mins

Components: 1 cup pomegranate juice, 1 banana, 1 cup oat milk

Serves: 1

Cooking technique: Blending

Steps: Blend pomegranate juice, a peeled banana, and oat milk until smooth.

Nutritional composition: Fat: 2g, Protein: 4g, Carbs: 35g, Rich in Antioxidants, High in Potassium.

Calories: 210

Recipe 6: Kiwi Quencher

Prep time: 5 mins

Components: 2 kiwis, 1 cup cold green tea, 1 tbsp honey

Serves: 1

Cooking technique: Blending

Steps: Peel kiwis and blend with cold green tea. Add honey and continue to blend until it is thoroughly mixed into the smoothie to prevent it from settling at the bottom.

Nutritional composition: Fat: 0.5g, Protein: 2g, Carbs: 25g, High in Vitamin C, Loaded with Antioxidants.

Calories: 120

Recipe 7: Peachy Keen

Prep time: 5 mins

Components: 2 peaches, 1 cup almond milk, 1 tsp flaxseeds

Serves: 1

Cooking technique: Blending

Steps: Blend peaches and almond milk until smooth. Add flaxseeds and pulse briefly to integrate them while maintaining their texture, providing a subtle crunch.

Nutritional composition: Fat: 3g, Protein: 2g, Carbs: 20g, High in Fiber, Good Source of Vitamin A.

Calories: 110

Recipe 8: Watermelon Wonder

Prep time: 5 mins

Components: 2 cups watermelon, 1 cup coconut water

Serves: 2

Cooking technique: Blending

Steps: Combine watermelon and coconut water; blend until achieving a light, refreshing consistency.

Nutritional composition: Fat: 0.2g, Protein: 1g, Carbs: 15g per serving, Excellent Hydration, Vitamin A: 30% DV.

Calories: 80 per serving

Recipe 9: Apricot Almond Elixir

Prep time: 5 mins

Components: 3 apricots, 1 cup almond milk, 1 tbsp maple syrup
Serves: 1
Cooking technique: Blending
Steps: Add pitted apricots, almond milk, and maple syrup to a blender and mix until the texture is uniformly creamy.
Nutritional composition: Fat: 2g, Protein: 2g, Carbs: 30g, High in Vitamin A, Good Source of Calcium.
Calories: 150

Recipe 10: Choco-Hazelnut Delight

Prep time: 6 mins
Components: 1 tbsp cocoa powder, 1 cup hazelnut milk, 1 tbsp agave syrup
Serves: 1
Cooking technique: Blending
Steps: Combine cocoa powder, hazelnut milk, and agave syrup in a blender; mix until perfectly smooth.
Nutritional composition: Fat: 4g, Protein: 2g, Carbs: 20g, High in Iron, Rich in Vitamin E.
Calories: 170

Recipe 11: Pear-Fection

Prep time: 5 mins
Components: 2 ripe pears, 1 cup rice milk, 1 tsp cinnamon
Serves: 2
Cooking technique: Blending
Steps: Peel and core the pears, then blend with rice milk and cinnamon for a smooth, evenly textured smoothie.
Nutritional composition: Fat: 0.5g, Protein: 1g, Carbs: 30g per serving, High in Fiber, Rich in Vitamin C.
Calories: 180 per serving

Recipe 12: Lemon-Lime Lift

Prep time: 5 mins
Components: Juice of 2 lemons and 2 limes, 1 cup cold water, 2 tbsp agave syrup
Serves: 2
Cooking technique: Blending
Steps: Juice the lemons and limes. Combine freshly squeezed lemon and lime juice with cold water and agave syrup; blend until fully integrated.
Nutritional composition: Fat: 0g, Protein: 0g, Carbs: 20g per serving, High in Vitamin C, Excellent for Hydration.
Calories: 90 per serving

Recipe 13: Raspberry Rhapsody

Prep time: 5 mins
Components: 1 cup raspberries, 1 cup oat milk, 1 tbsp chia seeds
Serves: 1
Cooking technique: Blending

Steps: Blend raspberries with oat milk until smooth. Add chia seeds and blend briefly to distribute them evenly through the mixture.
Nutritional composition: Fat: 4g, Protein: 3g, Carbs: 20g, High in Fiber, Rich in Vitamin C.
Calories: 150

Recipe 14: Avocado Allure

Prep time: 7 mins
Components: 1 avocado, 1 cup coconut milk, 1 tbsp honey
Serves: 1
Cooking technique: Blending
Steps: Peel and pit the avocado. Add avocado, coconut milk, and honey to the blender; mix until you achieve a creamy, luxurious texture.
Nutritional composition: Fat: 20g, Protein: 3g, Carbs: 20g, High in Healthy Fats, Rich in Potassium.
Calories: 320

Recipe 15: Vanilla Cherry Charm

Prep time: 5 mins
Components: 1 cup of pitted cherries, 1 cup almond milk, 1 tsp vanilla extract
Serves: 1
Cooking technique: Blending
Steps: Combine cherries, almond milk, and vanilla extract in a blender; blend until the mixture is velvety smooth.
Nutritional composition: Fat: 2g, Protein: 2g, Carbs: 20g, High in Antioxidants, Rich in Vitamin C.
Calories: 140

Recipe 16: Fig Fantasy

Prep time: 6 mins
Components: 5 fresh figs, 1 cup rice milk, 1 tbsp honey
Serves: 1
Cooking technique: Blending
Steps: Add fresh figs, rice milk, and honey to the blender; blend until smooth and uniform.
Nutritional composition: Fat: 1g, Protein: 2g, Carbs: 40g, High in Fiber, Good Source of Calcium.
Calories: 200

Recipe 17: Plum Perfection

Prep time: 5 mins
Components: 3 plums, 1 cup cold green tea, 1 tbsp agave syrup
Serves: 1
Cooking technique: Blending
Steps: Pit and slice the plums. Combine plums, cold green tea, and agave syrup in the blender. Blend until the plums are fully pureed and the mixture is smooth.

Nutritional composition: Fat: <1g, Protein: 1g, Carbs: 31g (natural sugars from plums and agave syrup)
High in antioxidants and vitamin C from plums.
Calories: 130

CHAPTER 10. 15 Detoxifying Daily Exercises

Daily exercises to enhance the detox effects of smoothies

Embarking on a journey to detoxify the body involves more than just nutrition; it requires a holistic approach that blends the rejuvenation of the mind, body, and soul. Engaging in specific exercises can amplify the detoxifying effects of the wholesome smoothies we've explored so far. Each exercise is carefully paired with a smoothie to harmonize the physical activity with nourishing rejuvenation.

1. Gentle Morning Yoga Stretch

Description:

Begin your day by revitalizing your body with a gentle yoga stretch routine, perfect for stimulating your circulation and aiding digestion. Stand with your feet about hip-width apart, grounding firmly through your heels and the balls of your feet. Allow your arms to hang loosely at your sides, fingers gently curled.

Take a deep breath in, and as you exhale, slowly raise your arms out to the side and overhead. With your arms reaching towards the sky, feel your spine lengthen and your body stretch upward from the ground.

As you take another deep breath in, prepare to fold forward. On your exhale, hinge at your hips and bend forward, keeping your spine straight as you go. Allow your hands to fall towards your feet; don't worry if they don't reach the ground – just let them hang as far as is comfortable, which might be your shins or knees.

On your next inhale, lift your torso halfway up, placing your hands on your thighs just above your knees. Keep your back flat, like a tabletop, and your gaze slightly forward to elongate your neck and spine.

Exhale as you release back into the forward fold, feeling a deep stretch down the back of your legs and along your spine.

To finish, inhale deeply and gradually roll back up to a standing position, letting your head and neck come up last. Repeat this flow of movements slowly for about 5 minutes, allowing the stretch to invigorate your body and prepare you for the day ahead.

Suggested Repetitions: Practice this sequence for 10 minutes each morning upon waking up.

Precautions: Ensure your movements are slow and controlled. If you have any back issues, bend your knees slightly during the forward bend to reduce strain.

Smoothie to Combine: Pair this exercise with the Citrus Sunrise to hydrate your body and invigorate your senses as you awaken.

2. Midday Breathing Meditation

Description:

Choose a quiet spot to sit comfortably with a straight back, either on a chair with feet flat on the ground or cross-legged on a cushion. Rest your hands on your knees, close your eyes, and begin to deepen your breath. Inhale through the nose for a count of four, filling your belly and chest with air. Hold your breath at the top for a count of four, then exhale slowly through the mouth for a count of six, releasing all the air and any tension. This practice of deep, rhythmic breathing helps to clear the mind and alleviate stress. It stimulates the parasympathetic nervous system, promoting a state of calm throughout your body. Regular practice can help to lower blood pressure, improve sleep, and enhance overall well-being.

Suggested Repetitions: Engage in this calming practice for 10 minutes during your midday break.

Precautions: Choose a comfortable seating position, ensuring there is no strain on the back or neck. Individuals with respiratory issues should consult a physician before engaging in breath control exercises.

Smoothie to Combine: This exercise pairs well with the Herbal Harmony, which can help reinforce the calming effects of deep breathing.

3. Evening Walk and Twist

Description:

An evening stroll is a fantastic way to decompress after a day's activities. Aim for a 15-minute walk at a moderate pace, allowing the rhythmic movement to clear your mind. Following your walk, perform standing torso twists to further aid digestion and unwind the body. Stand with feet hip-width apart, raise your arms to shoulder height, and gently twist your torso to the right, then to the left, letting your gaze follow the movement. This action helps to relax the spinal muscles and align the spine after a day of sitting or standing.

Suggested Repetitions: Indulge in a 15-minute walk followed by 5 minutes of gentle twisting in the evening.

Precautions: Ensure you are walking on even terrain to prevent tripping and keep the twists gentle to avoid any strain on the lower back.

Smoothie to Combine: Peachy Keen Sunrise complements this routine, with its antioxidant-rich components aiding in detoxification after your gentle evening activity.

4. Dynamic Lunges

Description:

Dynamic lunges engage the major muscles of the legs and hips. Stand with your feet together, step forward with your right foot, and lower your hips toward the floor until both knees are bent at a 90-degree angle. Make sure your front knee is directly above your ankle and your back knee is hovering just above the floor. Push through your right heel to return to the starting position, then repeat with the left leg. Perform three sets of 12 lunges on each leg, focusing on maintaining a straight back and engaged core throughout the movement.

Suggested Repetitions: Incorporate 3 sets of 12 lunges on each leg into your afternoon routine.

Precautions: Maintain proper alignment to avoid knee strain. Beginners can start with fewer repetitions.

Smoothie to Combine: Pair this exercise with the Spinach Tofu Energizer to replenish and support muscle recovery.

5. Nightly Gratitude Journaling and Stretching

Description:

End your day by reflecting on positive moments with gratitude journaling, which can be a powerful tool for mental clarity and stress reduction. After writing, transition into a stretching routine. Start with gentle neck rolls, then stretch your arms, torso, and legs. Pay particular attention to areas that hold tension, such as the shoulders and lower back. Hold each stretch for about 15 to 30 seconds, breathing deeply to enhance the relaxation effect. This combined practice can help in releasing both physical and emotional tension, preparing you for restorative sleep.

Suggested Repetitions: Spend 10 minutes on journaling and 10 minutes on stretching each night.

Precautions: Ensure your stretches are gentle and do not strain any muscles before sleep.

Smoothie to Combine: The Vanilla Snowflake is a perfect companion, promoting relaxation and aiding in nighttime detoxification.

6. Morning Sun Salutations

Description:

Sun Salutations, or Surya Namaskar, is a series of yoga poses performed in a continuous flow, traditionally practiced at sunrise. Start by standing tall, then fold forward, transition to a plank position, lower down, and rise into a cobra or upward-facing dog pose. Reverse the sequence back to a standing position. This ritual increases blood circulation, stimulates the digestive system, and enhances flexibility.

Suggested Repetitions: Begin your day with 5 rounds of Sun Salutations.

Precautions: Maintain proper form to avoid straining your back and shoulders. Those with existing health conditions should consult a physician.

Smoothie to Combine: Kickstart your morning with the Green Machine Medley, invigorating your senses.

7. Hydrating Aqua Aerobics

Description:

Water aerobics provides a full-body workout with minimal impact on the joints. In waist-deep water, perform exercises like high knees, leg kicks, and arm sweeps. The resistance of the water increases the intensity of the movements while also providing support. This form of exercise is excellent for improving strength, flexibility, and cardiovascular health, with the added benefit of being gentle on the body.

Suggested Repetitions: Engage in a 30-minute session of Aqua Aerobics in the early evening.

Precautions: Ensure the water is at a safe and comfortable depth and temperature.

Smoothie to Combine: Refresh post-exercise with the Watermelon Whisper, keeping your body hydrated and replenished.

8. Deep Stretching and Foam Rolling

Description:

Incorporate deep static stretches to lengthen the muscles and improve flexibility. Use a foam roller to apply pressure on tight muscles and fascia, particularly targeting the calves, hamstrings, quadriceps, and back. Slowly roll back and forth over each area for about 30 seconds to 1 minute, pausing at points of tension. This combination of stretching and rolling is excellent for post-workout recovery, improving blood flow, and reducing muscle soreness.

Suggested Repetitions: Incorporate a 20-minute session into your post-workout routine.

Precautions: Roll gently and avoid any areas of injury or extreme discomfort.

Smoothie to Combine: The Cherry Almond Bliss can aid in recovery and reduce muscle inflammation.

9. Energizing Dance Cardio

Description:

Dance Cardio involves free-form or choreographed dance movements that elevate the heart rate. Move rhythmically to your favorite tunes, allowing the beats to guide your body in dynamic motion. This form of cardio aids in calorie burning and toxin elimination through sweat.

Suggested Repetitions: Let loose for a 30-minute dance session in the afternoon.

Precautions: Wear comfortable footwear and ensure the space is free of obstacles.

Smoothie to Combine: Revitalize with the Tropical Sunshine Burst, bringing a burst of energy.

10. Tranquil Evening Tai Chi

Description:

Tai Chi, often referred to as "meditation in motion," is an ancient Chinese martial art that combines deep breathing with a series of movements performed in a slow, focused manner. Each posture flows into the next without pause, ensuring that your body is in constant motion.

To begin your Tai Chi practice in the evening, find a quiet and open space that allows you to move freely. Stand with your feet shoulder-width apart, knees slightly bent, and arms at your sides. Relax your shoulders and take a few deep breaths to center yourself.

Start with the "Warming Up the Qi" exercise. Gently bounce on your knees to awaken your energy channels. After a few bounces, come to a still position.

Move into "Opening the Chest." Inhale and gently sweep your arms out to the sides and then overhead, palms facing each other. As you exhale, bring your palms down in front of you as if pressing down on a large balloon, feeling the resistance. This helps open up your chest and gets the blood flowing.

Next, perform the "Wave Hands Like Clouds" movement. Extend one arm out at shoulder height and slowly pass your other hand across your body at waist level, as if your hands are clouds drifting across the sky. Shift your weight from one leg to the other in sync with your hands, turning your waist as you go. This movement promotes relaxation and mental tranquility.

Continue with the "Repulse Monkey" exercise. Imagine pushing something away from your chest with one hand while the other hand sweeps back behind you, as if you are pulling a rope. Step back with the corresponding leg as you do this, maintaining a slow and graceful pace. This exercise is excellent for improving coordination and balance.

Conclude your practice with the "Gathering the Earth and Sky" exercise. Inhale and pretend to gather energy from the earth with one hand while the other hand reaches to pull energy from the sky. Exhale as you bring both hands towards your belly, harmonizing the energies. Repeat this several times to center your body and spirit.

Suggested Repetitions: Go through each of these movements slowly and mindfully, spending about 4 minutes on each, to complete a 20-minute session. The goal is to focus on your breath and the fluidity of the movements rather than the number of repetitions.

Precautions: Tai Chi should be performed in a relaxed manner. If you feel any strain or discomfort, reduce the intensity of the movements. Make sure you have enough space to move without obstacles and wear comfortable clothing that allows for flexibility.

Smoothie to Combine: After your Tai Chi session, enjoying the Lemon Lush smoothie can be wonderfully refreshing. Its citrus elements and smooth texture provide a calming effect, complementing the serenity achieved through your exercises and assisting with digestion and relaxation before bedtime.

11. Dynamic High-Intensity Interval Training (HIIT)
Description:

Dynamic High-Intensity Interval Training is a structured pattern of high-energy exercises followed by short periods of rest or low-intensity activity. Examples include 30 seconds of sprinting followed by 30 seconds of walking, or doing jump squats for 45 seconds and then holding a plank for 15 seconds. This intense alternation not only torches calories but also increases your metabolic rate for hours post-exercise, aiding in detoxification and fat loss.

Suggested Repetitions: Incorporate a 20-minute HIIT session into your mid-morning routine.

Precautions: Wear supportive footwear and modify exercises as needed to avoid overexertion.

Smoothie to Combine: Replenish your energy with the Berry Quinoa Boost, restoring vitality after an intense workout.

12. Gentle Pilates Core Workout

Description:

Pilates is a mindful exercise that emphasizes body alignment and controlled breathing while performing a series of movements designed to strengthen the core muscles. A typical session might involve a precise series of the Pilates Five, which includes single-leg stretches, double-leg stretches, scissor kicks, double-leg lowers, and criss-cross exercises. These movements help to enhance core strength and stability, improve posture, and support efficient detoxification.

Suggested Repetitions: Engage in a 30-minute Pilates session in the afternoon.

Precautions: Maintain proper alignment and engage your core to protect your back.

Smoothie to Combine: The Kiwi Kale Edamame Charge complements this workout, nourishing your body from within.

13. Restorative Evening Walk

Description:

A restorative evening walk should not be just a casual stroll; it should be purposeful and mindful. Use this time to engage with your surroundings, practicing deep breathing and mindfulness to enhance the detoxifying benefits. Pay attention to the rhythm of your steps and the natural environment around you. This form of gentle exercise aids in digestion and helps to clear the mind, reducing stress levels, which is vital for overall detoxification.

Suggested Repetitions: End your day with a calming 30-minute walk.

Precautions: Wear comfortable shoes and stay in well-lit areas.

Smoothie to Combine: Pair this exercise with the Cinnamon Apple Crisp, easing you into relaxation.

14. Meditative Breathing Exercises

Description:

Meditative breathing exercises are simple yet powerful practices that focus on controlling the breath to calm the mind and relax the body. They can be practiced by anyone, regardless of experience with meditation or yoga.

Start with a basic diaphragmatic breathing to establish a calm rhythm:
- Find a quiet space where you can sit or lie down comfortably without interruptions.
- Place one hand on your chest and the other on your abdomen.
- Breathe in slowly through your nose, allowing your stomach to rise as much as feels comfortable. Your chest should move only slightly while your abdomen expands.
- Exhale gently through your mouth or nose, letting your stomach slowly fall. Try to make your exhale twice as long as you inhale.

Once you feel comfortable with diaphragmatic breathing, incorporate the following techniques to enhance your meditative practice:

Bee Breath (Soothing Hum):
- Close your eyes and relax your face.
- Inhale deeply through your nose.
- As you exhale, gently close your ears with your index fingers and make a soft humming sound like a bee. The vibration is soothing and can help quiet the mind.

Skull Shining Breath (Energizing):
- Sit with your spine straight and your hands on your knees.
- Take a passive inhale through your nose.
- Exhale forcefully through your nose, contracting your abdominal muscles to push the air out.
- Let your lungs automatically refill with air for the next round.
- Start with 10 breaths, gradually increasing as you feel comfortable.

Alternate Nostril Breathing (Balancing):

Sit comfortably with your back straight.
- Place your left hand on your knee and your right thumb gently on your right nostril.
- Close your right nostril and inhale slowly through the left nostril.

- Pause at the top of the inhale, release your right nostril, and close the left nostril with your ring finger.
- Exhale slowly through the right nostril, then inhale through the same nostril.
- Pause, switch nostrils, and repeat the cycle for several rounds.

Suggested Repetitions: Begin with 3-5 minutes for each technique, gradually building up to a 10-minute session in the morning and evening.

Precautions: Ensure you're sitting comfortably in a place where you won't be disturbed. Never force your breath, and if you feel dizzy or uncomfortable, pause and return to normal breathing. Those with respiratory conditions or pregnant women should consult with a healthcare provider before attempting these exercises.

Smoothie to Combine: The Minty Pineapple Paradise pairs well, promoting internal freshness and clarity.

15. Strength-Building Bodyweight Exercises

Description:

Strength-building bodyweight exercises should be executed with precision and control. An effective routine could include 3 sets of 10 squats, 10 push-ups, and 10 lunges on each leg, followed by a core set of 15-second planks, side planks, and back extensions. These exercises not only help build muscle and burn fat but also improve metabolic function and support the body's natural detoxification pathways by enhancing circulation and lymphatic flow.

Suggested Repetitions: Engage in a 25-minute session of bodyweight exercises in the early evening.

Precautions: Maintain proper form to avoid straining muscles and joints.

Smoothie to Combine: The Protein Powerhouse is a perfect companion, aiding muscle recovery and providing sustained energy.

CHAPTER 11 - 4-Week Detoxifying Meal Plan and Preparation

Week 1 Plan

Day	Breakfast	Lunch	Dinner
Monday	Blooming Berry Bliss	Verdant Zest	Green Machine Medley
Tuesday	Tropical Sunshine Burst	Herbal Harmony	Fresh Mint Mirage
Wednesday	Spiced Pumpkin Pleasure	Green Zen	Celery Serenity
Thursday	Citrus Sunrise	Spring Sprout	Pineapple Paradise
Friday	Kiwi Kale Kickstart	Asparagus Ascend	Fennel Fusion
Saturday	Cherry Almond Bliss	Celery Citrus Sip	Beetroot Bliss
Sunday	Omega-Raspberry Elixir	Pea & Mint Magic	Radiant Raspberry

Week 1 Shopping List

Ingredients	Quantity for week 1
Bananas	7
Mixed berries	4 cups
Mangoes	2
Peaches	4
Watermelon	1 small
Pomegranate seeds	1 cup
Apples	4
Oranges	7
Pineapples	1 medium
Cherries	1 cup
Spinach	4 cups
Kale	4 cups
Celery	2 stalks
Beetroot	2
Carrots	4 medium
Cucumber	2 medium
Greek yogurt	4 cups
Protein powder	According to need
Nut butters	1 cup
Almond milk	1 gallon
Coconut water	4 cups
Honey	1 small jar
Maple syrup	1 small jar
Vanilla extract	1 bottle
Cinnamon	1 container
Chia seeds	1 bag
Flaxseeds	1 bag
Acai powder	1 package
Matcha powder	1 package
Hemp seeds	1 bag

Week 2 Plan

Day	Breakfast	Lunch	Dinner
Monday	Peachy Keen Sunrise	Berry Bliss Burst	Tropical Harmony
Tuesday	Zesty Lemon Quencher	Mango Melody	Berry Bliss with Acai

Wednesday	Creamy Cacao Cool-off	Sunlit Citrus Splash	Peachy Serenity
Thursday	Watermelon Wonder	Kiwi & Kale Dance	Citrus Glow
Friday	Pomegranate Passion	Passionfruit Paradise	Cherry Charm with Goji
Saturday	Energizing Beet Boost	Cool Cucumber Melange	Watermelon Whisper
Sunday	Nutmeg Nectar	Papaya Peach Fusion	Sunset Serenade

Week 2 shopping list

Ingredients	Quantity for Week 2
Mixed Berries (frozen or fresh)	4 cups
Bananas	7
Mangoes	2
Peaches	4
Spinach	2 bunches
Kale	1 bunch
Celery	1 stalk
Cucumbers	2
Almond milk	2 quarts
Coconut water	1 quart
Greek yogurt	2 cups
Protein powder	1 container (as needed)
Chia seeds	1/4 cup
Flax seeds	1/4 cup
Honey	1 small jar
Pomegranate seeds	1 cup
Watermelon	1 small
Avocados	3

Ginger root	1 small piece
Lemons	4
Apples	4
Oranges	3
Pineapples	1
Mint leaves	1 bunch
Parsley	1 bunch
Beetroot	2
Carrots	4
Nut butter	1 jar
Coconut flakes	1/4 cup
Pumpkin seeds	1/4 cup
Spirulina powder	1 small packet
Acai berry powder	1 small packet
Ground turmeric	1 small bottle
Ground cinnamon	1 small bottle
Ground nutmeg	1 small bottle
Vanilla extract	1 small bottle

Week 3 Plan

Day	Breakfast	Lunch	Dinner
Monday	Spiced Pumpkin Pleasure	Autumn Maple Melody	Cinnamon Apple Crisp
Tuesday	Apple Pie Embrace	Apple Orchard Delight	Cozy Pumpkin Patch
Wednesday	Warm Ginger Zing	Cranberry Crush	Pecan Pie Dream
Thursday	Nutty Maple Hug	Fig & Date Symphony	Sweet Potato Comfort
Friday	Pear and Pecan Perfection	Nutty Butternut Bliss	Cranberry Cheer
Saturday	Cranberry Crimson Crush	Pecan Pie Smoothie	Toasty Hazelnut Heaven
Sunday	Sweet Potato Sunrise	Golden Persimmon Potion	Fig & Date Delight

Week 3 shopping list

Ingredients	Quantity for Week 3
Mixed Berries (frozen or fresh)	4 cups
Bananas	7
Mangoes	2
Peaches	4
Spinach	2 bunches
Kale	1 bunch
Celery	1 stalk
Cucumbers	2
Almond milk	2 quarts
Coconut water	1 quart
Greek yogurt	2 cups
Protein powder	As needed for servings
Chia seeds	1/4 cup
Flax seeds	1/4 cup
Honey	As needed
Pomegranate seeds	1 cup
Watermelon	1 small
Avocados	3
Ginger root	1 small piece
Lemons	4
Apples	4
Oranges	3
Pineapples	1
Mint leaves	1 bunch
Parsley	1 bunch
Beetroot	2
Carrots	4
Nut butter	As needed
Coconut flakes	1/4 cup
Pumpkin seeds	1/4 cup
Spirulina powder	1 small packet
Acai berry powder	1 small packet
Ground turmeric	1 small bottle
Ground cinnamon	1 small bottle
Ground nutmeg	1 small bottle
Vanilla extract	1 small bottle

Week 4 Plan

Day	Breakfast	Lunch	Dinner
Monday	Winterberry Warmth	Immunity Boosting Blend	Vanilla Snowflake
Tuesday	Peppermint Pep	Creamy Cacao Comfort	Minty Cocoa Comfort
Wednesday	Spicy Ginger Glow	Spicy Turmeric Tango	Citrus Winter Bliss
Thursday	Power Matcha Mix	Gingered Pear Perfection	Spiced Almond Joy
Friday	Cocoa Comfort	Energizing Espresso Elixir	Berry Winter Warmer
Saturday	Raspberry Revival	Walnut Wonder	Cozy Chocolate Cherry
Sunday	Guarana Gusto	Berry Citrus Symphony	Nutty Caramel Hug

Week 4 shopping list

Ingredients	Quantity for Week 4
Mixed Berries (frozen or fresh)	4 cups
Bananas	7
Mangoes	2
Peaches	4
Spinach	2 bunches
Kale	1 bunch
Celery	1 stalk
Cucumbers	2
Almond milk	2 quarts
Coconut water	1 quart
Greek yogurt	2 cups
Protein powder	As needed for servings
Chia seeds	1/4 cup
Flax seeds	1/4 cup
Honey	As needed
Pomegranate seeds	1 cup
Watermelon	1 small
Avocados	3
Ginger root	1 small piece
Lemons	4
Apples	4
Oranges	3
Pineapples	1
Mint leaves	1 bunch
Parsley	1 bunch
Beetroot	2
Carrots	4
Nut butter	As needed
Coconut flakes	1/4 cup
Pumpkin seeds	1/4 cup
Spirulina powder	1 small packet
Acai berry powder	1 small packet
Ground turmeric	1 small bottle
Ground cinnamon	1 small bottle
Ground nutmeg	1 small bottle
Vanilla extract	1 small bottle

Conclusion

In our journey through this guide, we have discovered the transformative power of smoothies, evolving from simple fruit mixtures to integral components of modern health and nutrition. Their appeal lies in the seamless fusion of wellness, convenience, and flavor, making them accessible to everyone, from the bustling professional to the health-conscious individual.

Smoothies represent the perfect blend of nutrition and versatility. With just a blender and a selection of fresh ingredients, anyone can create a personalized drink that is both nourishing and delicious. This guide has illustrated how each ingredient adds its unique touch, much like an artist's palette, allowing for a customized health masterpiece tailored to individual tastes and nutritional needs.

Beyond their delicious taste, smoothies are adaptable to various dietary goals and preferences. They can align with weight management, muscle building, detoxification, or simply boosting daily nutrient intake. Their ability to incorporate seasonal ingredients ensures every sip resonates with freshness and vitality.

From energizing breakfast blends to decadent dessert-like treats, the recipes we've explored offer a range of options for every palate. Smoothies are not just beverages; they are an exciting culinary journey, a blend of creativity and health.

This exploration of smoothies comes with a mindful approach to ingredient selection and a commitment to sustainable practices, ensuring our smoothie experience is beneficial for both us and the environment.

As we conclude, it's evident that smoothies are much more than just a health trend. They are a reflection of personal health goals and culinary preferences, transcending food to become a daily ritual of self-care. This guide has aimed to be your companion in this flavourful journey, inspiring you to explore the vast potential of smoothies.

In wrapping up this smoothie exploration, the shared adventures of blending and tasting carry on. It's the unique experiences and insights of every smoothie enthusiast and taster that add depth and color to this ongoing journey.

Embrace the world of smoothies as a celebration of nourishment and creativity. Whether you are an avid smoothie lover or just starting out, the journey is uniquely yours, filled with endless possibilities and flavors. Here's to a delightful path to wellness, rich in taste and health benefits.

Conversion table

Ingredient Type	U.S. Measurement	Metric Equivalent
Liquids		
Water/Milk/Juice	1 cup	240 ml
	1 tablespoon (tbsp.)	15 ml
	1 teaspoon (tsp)	5 ml
Dry Goods		
Flour/Sugar	1 cup	120 grams
	1 tablespoon (tbsp.)	14 grams
	1 teaspoon (tsp)	4.2 grams
Semi-solids		
Honey/Yogurt	1 cup	340 grams
	1 tablespoon (tbsp.)	21 grams
	1 teaspoon (tsp)	7 grams
Fats		
Butter/Oil	1 cup	227 grams
	1 tablespoon (tbsp.)	14 grams
	1 teaspoon (tsp)	4.7 grams
Small Measures		
Baking Powder/Soda	1 teaspoon (tsp)	4.2 grams
Salt	1 teaspoon (tsp)	5.7 grams
Temperature		
	325°F	165°C
	350°F	177°C
	375°F	190°C
	400°F	205°C
	425°F	220°C
Weight		
Cheese/Meat	1 pound (lb)	0.45 kilograms
	1 ounce (oz)	28 grams

Please note that for dry ingredients, the weight can vary significantly depending on the ingredient's density. For example, a cup of flour weighs less than a cup of sugar. Therefore, the metric equivalents provided are approximate and should be adjusted as necessary.

INDEX (Alphabetical Order)

Acai Awakening
Almond Chickpea Fusion
Apple Cinnamon Delight
Apple Orchard Delight
Apple Pie Embrace
Apricot Almond Elixir
Apricot Euphoria
Asparagus Ascend
Autumn Maple Melody
Avocado Allure
Avocado Almond Ambrosia
Avocado Aloe Elixir
Avocado Serenity
Beetroot Bliss
Beetroot Bliss
Beetroot Bliss
Berry Bliss Burst
Berry Bliss with Acai
Berry Citrus Symphony
Berry Protein Fusion
Berry Quinoa Boost
Berry Winter Warmer
Blooming Berry Bliss
Blueberry Basil Boost
Blueberry Basil Burst
Blueberry Blast
Blueberry Burst
Cacao Cashew Bliss
Caramel Apple Crave
Caramelized Pear Whisper
Carrot Ginger Glow

Cashew Charm
Celery Citrus Sip
Celery Serenity
Celery Symphony
Chai Chilled Charm
Chai-infused Pear Perfection
Charcoal Clarity
Cherry Almond Bliss
Cherry Charm with Goji
Chia Cherry Charge
Chilly Chaga Charm
Choco Almond Dream
Choco-Almond Delight
Choco-Banana Blossom
Choco-Hazelnut Delight
Cinnamon Apple Crisp
Cinnamon Cradle
Citrus Cleanse
Citrus Fat Burner
Citrus Glow
Citrus Sunrise
Citrus Symphony
Citrus Winter Bliss
Cocoa Almond Lift
Cocoa Comfort
Coconut Watermelon Wave
Cool Cucumber Melange
Cozy Chocolate Cherry
Cozy Pumpkin Patch
Cranberry Cheer
Cranberry Crimson Crush

Cranberry Crush
Creamy Cacao Comfort
Creamy Cacao Cool-off
Cucumber Calm
Dandelion Delight
Dandelion Detox
Energizing Beet Boost
Energizing Espresso Elixir
Fennel Freshness
Fennel Fusion
Fig & Date Delight
Fig & Date Symphony
Fig and Honey Harmony
Fig Fantasy
Floral Apricot Fusion
Fresh Mint Mirage
Ginger Glow
Gingerbread Embrace
Gingered Pear Perfection
Goji Grapefruit Goodness
Golden Grapefruit Glow
Golden Persimmon Potion
Greek Yogurt Citrus Zing
Green Apple Metabolism Booster
Green Machine
Green Machine Medley
Green Morning Revival
Green Tea Metabolism Mixer
Green Zen
Guarana Gusto
Guava Grace
Hazelnut Harmony
Herbal Harmony

Honey Berry Bliss
Immunity Boosting Blend
Kale and Kiwi Kickstart
Kale Kickstart
Kiwi & Kale Dance
Kiwi Kale Edamame Charge
Kiwi Kale Kickstart
Kiwi Kiss
Kiwi Quencher
Lavender Love Smoothie
Lemon Lush
Lemon-Lime Lift
Lychee Luxury
Mango Melody
Mango Tango
Maple Walnut Warmth
Matcha Magic
Matcha Mint Marvel
Minty Cocoa Comfort
Minty Cucumber Refresher
Minty Melon Refresh
Minty Pineapple Paradise
Minty Watermelon Wave
Mocha Hemp Elevation
Mocha Motivator
Nutmeg Nectar
Nutty Butternut Bliss
Nutty Caramel Hug
Nutty Maple Hug
Oatmeal Cinnamon Protein Rush
Omega-Raspberry Elixir
Papaya Passion
Papaya Peach Fusion

Parsley Purity
Passionfruit Paradise
Pea & Mint Magic
Peach Perfection
Peachy Keen
Peachy Keen Sunrise
Peachy Protein Power
Peachy Serenity
Peanut Butter Banana Delight
Pear & Ginger Soothe
Pear and Pecan Perfection
Pear-Fection
Pecan Pie Dream
Pecan Pie Smoothie
Peppermint Pep
Pineapple Coconut Oasis
Pineapple Paradise
Pineapple Paradise
Pineapple Purity
Pineapple Spirulina Surge
Pineapple Tempeh Triumph
Pistachio Pleasure
Plum Passion
Plum Perfection
Pomegranate Passion with juice
Pomegranate Passion with seeds
Pomegranate Peace
Pomegranate Pumpkin Seed Punch
Pomegranate Purity
Power Matcha Mix
Protein Petal Punch
Protein Powerhouse
Protein Pumpkin Patch

Pumpkin Pleasure
Radiant Raspberry
Raspberry Chia Harmony
Raspberry Rapture
Raspberry Refresher
Raspberry Revival
Raspberry Rhapsody
Refreshing Watermelon Wave
Savory Spinach and Avocado
Simple Berry Bliss
Soy Berry Bliss
Spiced Almond Joy
Spiced Carrot Cake
Spiced Pumpkin Pleasure
Spicy Avocado Slimmer
Spicy Carrot Cooler
Spicy Ginger Glow
Spicy Ginger Pineapple
Spicy Ginger Protein Kick
Spicy Mango Tango
Spicy Turmeric Tango
Spinach Tofu Energizer
Spirulina Surge
Spring Basil Bliss
Spring Melon Medley
Spring Sprout
Strawberry Basil Booster
Strawberry Sunrise
Sunlit Citrus Splash
Sunset Serenade
Sweet Beet Retreat
Sweet Potato Comfort
Sweet Potato Euphoria

Sweet Potato Sunrise
Sweet Spinach Slimmer
Toasty Hazelnut Heaven
Tropical Harmony
Tropical Lentil Bliss
Tropical Sunshine Burst
Tropical Triumph
Tropical Turmeric Tonic
Tropical Zest
Turmeric Ginger Soothe
Turmeric Tonic
Turmeric Twist
Vanilla Cherry Charm
Vanilla Snowflake

Vanilla Velvet
Verdant Zest
Walnut Wonder with banana
Walnut Wonder with kefir
Warm Ginger Zing
Watercress Wonder
Watermelon Whisper
Watermelon Wonder
Winterberry Warmth
Zesty Cherry Chill
Zesty Lemon Cleanse
Zesty Lemon Quencher
Zesty Lime Lullaby

Made in the USA
Las Vegas, NV
28 June 2024